RISE *And* LEAD

REIGNITE, REINVENT, AND SUCCEED IN YOUR MID-CAREER JOURNEY

NAGARAJU SIDDAM

ISBN
Paperback 979-8-89632-333-4
Hardcase 979-8-89673-809-1

Contents

Foreword   *9*

Introduction:
Your Journey and Why This Book Matters   *11*

Part 1   **Recognizing and Navigating the**
                 Mid-Career Plateau   **15**

Chapter 1   Understanding the Mid-Career Plateau   16

             Identifying career stagnation in the fast-paced IT world   18

             Personal Reflections and Anecdotes on Facing Career
             Stagnation   25

             Common Challenges and Fears Faced by Mid-Career
             Professionals   28

Chapter 2   Embracing Change and Uncertainty   32

             The Power of Mindset Shifts in Career Transitions   33

             Overcoming Fear: The First Step to Reinvention   39

             Embracing Change: A Personal Journey in the
             Tech World   41

Part 2	**Defining Your Career Direction**	**49**
Chapter 3	Defining Your Vision, Mission, and Goals	50
	Crafting Clarity: A Guide for Mid-Career Professionals	51
	Aligning Personal and Professional Objectives for Lasting Success	59
Chapter 4	Personal Branding and Visibility	66
	Why Personal Branding is Key to Thriving in the IT Industry	67
	Building Visibility and Influence with Key Decision-Makers	72
	Strategies for Increasing Your Visibility Within Your Company and in the Industry	76

Part 3	**Building Leadership and Managing Teams**	**81**
Chapter 5	Developing Leadership Traits and Managing Teams	82
	Key Leadership Traits Every IT Professional Should Master	83
	Transitioning from Individual Contributor to Leader	89
Chapter 6	Continuous Learning and Staying Relevant	91
	The Importance of Staying Updated in a Rapidly Evolving Tech Landscape	92
	Identifying the Right Learning Paths, Skills, and Certifications	97
	Balancing Continuous Learning with Day-to-Day Responsibilities	101

Part 4 **Overcoming Challenges and Pushing Boundaries** **107**

Chapter 7 Self-Development and Building the Right Habits 108

The habits of successful mid-career IT professionals. 109

Developing a growth-oriented mindset: 114

Emotional Intelligence: The Bedrock of Self-Development and Leadership 121

How to Manage Time, Energy, and Focus Effectively – The 4-Letter Framework 128

Chapter 8 Getting Out of Your Comfort Zone 133

Breaking Free from Career Stagnation by Embracing New Challenges 134

Practical Steps to Push Beyond Your Comfort Zone for Exponential Growth 141

Chapter 9 Overcoming Setbacks and Building Resilience 147

Embracing Career Failures and Learning from Them 148

Strategies for Recovering from Career Setbacks 157

Building Resilience and Staying Focused in Challenging Environments. 161

Part 5 **Long-Term Success and Organizational Impact** **167**

Chapter 10 Leading Organizational Transformation 168

Leading Positive Change: A Journey of Empowerment and Growth 169

Fostering a Culture of Excellence and Continuous Improvement 172

Practical Strategies for Driving Innovation and
Organizational Growth   178

Chapter 11   Future-Proofing Your Career for
Long-Term Success   186

Preparing for Future Challenges in Leadership and
Tech   187

Aligning Personal Growth with Future Industry
Trends   191

How to Build a Sustainable, Thriving Career in the
Ever-Evolving IT Industry   196

Conclusion: Your Journey Ahead   *201*

Acknowledgments   *207*

About the Author   *209*

References   *210*

Dedication

To my beloved parents (Kishan and Sujatha), whose love, sacrifices, and values continue to guide me even in their absence.

This book, *Rise and Lead: Reignite, Reinvent, and Succeed in Your Mid-Career Journey*, is a testament to the lessons you instilled in me—resilience, hard work, and the courage to rise again.

Your unwavering belief in my potential fuels my every step, and this journey is as much a reflection of your legacy as it is of my experiences.

With eternal love and gratitude, this book is dedicated to you.

Foreword

If you have ever found yourself at a crossroads in your career, feeling stagnant or uncertain about your next steps, then *"Rise and Lead: Reignite, Reinvent, and Succeed in Your Mid-Career Journey"* by Nagaraju Siddam is your essential guide. This book is designed to help you navigate the challenges of mid-career transitions in the fast-paced IT industry, offering insights and strategies to reignite your professional journey.

As a Mind Performance Coach and the author of the bestseller 'Unleash the Power of Reading', I understand the importance of self-awareness and growth in achieving career success. The mid-career plateau can be daunting, but it is also an opportunity for profound transformation. This book provides the tools you need to recognize when it is time to make a change and to embrace the uncertainty that comes with it.

Throughout *'Rise and Lead: Reignite, Reinvent, and Succeed in Your Mid-Career Journey'* book, you will explore how to define your vision, set strategic goals, and build a personal brand that stands out in the competitive IT landscape. You will learn practical strategies for developing leadership qualities and managing high-performing teams while balancing the demands of continuous learning in a rapidly evolving tech world.

This journey is not just about overcoming challenges; it is about pushing boundaries and cultivating resilience. The stories and experiences shared in this book will inspire you to step outside your comfort zone and embrace the opportunities that lie ahead.

Whether you are feeling stuck, seeking advancement, or ready to take the next leap in your career, *"Rise and Lead: Reignite, Reinvent, and Succeed in Your Mid-Career Journey"* is here to support you. If you are prepared to transform your mid-career plateau into a launching pad for success, this book will be your trusted companion. Together, let's unlock your full potential and pave the way for a fulfilling and impactful career in technology.

Best wishes,

(Dr. Manjunath M.S.)

Mind Performance Coach and Author of 'Unleash the Power of Reading'.

Introduction: Your Journey and Why This Book Matters

My journey in the tech industry has been a mosaic of learning, challenges, and growth—each experience shaping me into the leader I am today. I started my career as a software engineer, driven by a deep curiosity for technology and a desire to create solutions that make a difference. As I navigated through various roles, from product development to program management, and ultimately into organizational development, I found myself increasingly fascinated by the broader impact of strategic initiatives and people management.

Over time, my role expanded beyond the technical, and I began leading teams across the globe, establishing Centers of Excellence, and driving innovation and efficiency in product lines. The transition from being an individual contributor to a leader was not always straightforward. It was filled with moments of self-doubt, intense learning curves, and the constant challenge of balancing vision with execution. But it was also incredibly rewarding. I discovered that leadership is not just about managing tasks; it is about inspiring people, fostering a culture of excellence, and creating an environment where innovation can thrive.

Midway through my career, I reached a crossroads—what many might call the mid-career plateau. It is a phase where the initial excitement of early career successes starts to wane, and the weight of higher responsibilities becomes more pronounced. Yet, I realized that this was also a pivotal moment—a chance to redefine my path, leverage my accumulated experience, and make an even greater impact. It became clear to me that mid-career is not about maintaining the status quo; it is about reinvention, strategic growth, and stepping into leadership roles that shape the future of our industry.

This realization is what compelled me to write this book. I have seen many talented professionals, particularly in the software industry, struggle with this transition. The fast-paced, ever-evolving nature of tech makes mid-career transitions uniquely challenging. But it is also within this complexity that the greatest opportunities lie. This book is my way of sharing the insights I have gained, the strategies that have guided me, and the lessons learned from leading teams, driving change, and navigating my own mid-career journey.

In '*Rise and Lead: Reignite, Reinvent, and Succeed in Your Mid-Career Journey*', I will walk you through transforming the mid-career plateau into a launching pad for your next big leap. You will discover how to build and lead high-performing teams, establish Centers of Excellence that drive innovation and new product development, and navigate the intricate balance between strategic vision and operational execution. I will also share stories from my own experiences—moments of triumph and setback, and how they contributed to my growth as a leader.

Recognizing and Navigating the Mid-Career Plateau

Chapter 1

Understanding the Mid-Career Plateau

1. Identifying career stagnation in the fast-paced IT world.

2. Common fears and challenges faced by mid-career professionals.

3. Recognizing when and how to make changes to regain momentum

4. Take a moment...and Ask yourself below questions to understand your current state:

- **Have you reached a point in your career where success feels routine, but the excitement and growth you once felt seem to be fading?**

- **Are you finding yourself questioning whether your current role truly reflects your full potential or wondering if there's something more waiting beyond your comfort zone?**

- Do you feel like you have mastered your technical expertise but struggle to see a clear path for growth or advancement in your current role?

- As the IT landscape evolves rapidly, are you questioning whether your current career trajectory still aligns with where you want to be in the next 5-10 years?

Identifying career stagnation in the fast-paced IT world

A mid-career plateau is a phase many professionals encounter, often without realizing it until the signs have already taken root. It does not come crashing into your career—it sneaks in quietly, hiding beneath the surface of your daily routines. The excitement that once defined your work begins to fade, replaced by a growing sense of monotony. The learning that previously fueled your professional journey slows, and you find yourself questioning your purpose. The very work that was once a source of passion becomes mechanical, and the drive to achieve seems to dwindle.

I personally experienced this during a pivotal moment in my career. After several years of successfully leading projects, managing global teams, and driving initiatives as part of a Center of Excellence, I noticed that the energy I once brought to the table was slowly fading. Initially, I did not recognize the subtle shifts. My learning curve, once steep and thrilling, had flattened. Tasks I once found challenging became routine, and projects that had once ignited my creative thinking now felt like a mere checkbox on my to-do list. The passion I once had for each new challenge slowly ebbed away.

For a long time, I convinced myself that it was just a temporary lull – that the thrill would return. But it did not. I started to feel stagnant. Despite having achieved much in my career, I could no longer ignore the creeping realization that I was not growing. I began to ask myself, "What's next?" The goals I had set for myself earlier in my career felt distant and less urgent, replaced by a fog of uncertainty.

Feeling Stuck in Tech? You are Not Alone.

It creeps up on you when you least expect it. You are in the flow, leading projects, managing teams, and feeling like you have got your career on track. Then, one day, it hits you—the excitement is gone. The challenges that once kept you up at night, brainstorming solutions, are now just boxes to check. The passion that fueled your drive to succeed seems to have quietly slipped away, leaving you to wonder, *"Is this it?"*

I have been there. After years of pushing myself—managing global teams, spearheading initiatives, and solving complex problems—I coasted. I did not recognize it at first. I was still getting the job done, but the spark was missing. I convinced myself it was just a phase, that the thrill would come back with the next big project. But it did not. Slowly, I realized my learning curve had flattened. The work that once inspired me now felt mechanical, and I was not growing.

The worst part? I was not sure what to do next. My goals, once so clear and ambitious, now felt distant, like a faded memory. The uncertainty left me feeling stuck, and I questioned if I would plateau for good.

Emotionally, I felt like I was at a crossroads—do I keep going, settling into this comfort zone? Or do I take the risk of stepping into the unknown to reignite my career? Psychologically, the fear of failure loomed large, but staying stagnant felt worse.

If you are feeling this way, know you are not alone. The mid-career plateau is real, but it is not the end. It is a signal to pause, reflect, and redefine what success looks like for you now. It is your opportunity to rediscover your purpose, challenge yourself, and reignite the passion that once drove you. If you have ever found yourself in a similar position, know that you are not alone. Many mid-career professionals, especially in tech, hit this plateau. But this is also an opportunity—a moment to pause, reflect, and redefine your path forward. It is a signal to start rewriting your story, reigniting your passion, and embracing the next phase of your journey with renewed purpose.

Subtle Signs of a Mid-Career Plateau

It creeps in quietly—a mid-career plateau. On the surface, everything seems fine. You are still performing, still contributing, and still checking all the boxes. But something inside feels different. There's a subtle dissatisfaction, an undercurrent of restlessness you cannot quite explain. I know because I have been there. It is not a sudden crash, but a slow, silent slide into stagnation.

1. **Diminished Excitement**: Remember when every new project lit a fire in you? You stayed late, thought creatively, and felt a rush with every challenge. Now, even new assignments feel predictable, and that spark of excitement is hard to find.

2. **Growth Stalls**: Once, your learning curve was steep. You were constantly absorbing new skills and stretching

yourself. But now, things feel flat. The work that used to inspire growth feels routine. You wonder if you are learning anything new at all.

3. **Comfort Becomes Complacency**: Comfort can be a silent trap. At some point, you stop pushing yourself. The hunger to innovate and go beyond the norm fades. You are still doing your job, but the drive to excel has dimmed.

4. **Foggy Future**: Once, you had a clear vision of where you were headed. Now, your direction feels blurry. Questions like, *What is next? Am I on the right path?* cloud your mind and the ambitions that once drove you feel distant.

5. **Energy Drains**: This might be the most telling sign. The enthusiasm that once propelled you out of bed each morning has waned. You are going through the motions, but without that inner spark that once defined your passion for work.

I have walked this path—waking up one day, realizing the growth and excitement had faded. It hit me hard. But this plateau is not a dead end—it is a call to reflect, reignite, and rediscover your purpose. If you have felt any of these signs, you are not alone. It is time to act.

Realizing the Plateau

Recognizing you are stuck on a career plateau is often the hardest step. For me, it came after more than three years in the same leadership role. I started with enthusiasm, driven by the excitement of leading global teams, navigating complex projects, and pushing new initiatives. But over time, the spark faded. What once felt like a growth opportunity became routine. I was not failing, but I was not growing either. I was doing well—yet, *well* was not enough anymore.

Many of us reach this point without even realizing it. You're comfortable, you're successful, but there's an inner voice asking, *"Is this all there is?"* It is easy to mistake this comfort for success, but beneath it lies complacency. That steep climb you once thrived on begins to flatten, and before you know it, you are on a plateau.

This experience is not unique. Consider Howard Schultz, the visionary behind Starbucks. Early in his career, he faced a plateau while working for a coffee equipment company, feeling limited in his ability to innovate and grow. That realization pushed him to take a leap of faith, acquiring Starbucks and transforming it into a global phenomenon. His story exemplifies how moments of stagnation can serve as catalysts for entrepreneurial breakthroughs and meaningful reinvention.

Indra Nooyi, former CEO of PepsiCo, also faced a mid-career plateau. After years in strategic roles, she found herself no longer learning. A bold shift into a broader, visionary role reignited her growth, ultimately leading her to greater global success.

If you have felt this stagnation, know that it is not the end; it is an opportunity to reflect and redefine your career trajectory.

Breaking Free from the Plateau

Recognizing you are on a career plateau is hard, but the real challenge is figuring out how to break free. For me, it was realizing that my comfort zone was holding me back. Sure, it felt safe and familiar, but that same comfort was keeping me away from growing. I knew that if I wanted more from my career, I needed to push myself beyond the boundaries of what I already knew.

Here are five strategies that helped me—and can help you—reignite your career when it feels stuck:

1. **Pursue New Learning**

   When your skills feel stagnant, it is a sign to invest in your growth. Enroll in courses, attend workshops, or seek out mentorship from someone outside your immediate circle. Learning something new not only keeps you relevant but reignites that curiosity and drive that may have faded over time. For me, finding a mentor in a completely different area of expertise opened my mind to new possibilities.

2. **Expand Your Role**

   Growth does not always mean leaving your job. Sometimes, it is about finding new challenges within your current role. Take on responsibilities that stretch you—lead a cross-functional project or spearhead a new initiative. When I took on a role outside my comfort zone, I found myself reenergized and engaged in ways I had not been in years.

3. **Revisit Your Goals**

Sometimes, plateaus happen because you have lost sight of what truly drives you. Take a step back and ask yourself: *What do I want from my career?* When I reassessed my long-term goals, I realized I had drifted from what truly mattered to me. That clarity gave me the purpose I needed to move forward.

4. **Network with Leaders**

Talk to people who have been there before. Reach out to industry leaders and colleagues who have navigated similar plateaus. Their stories can provide insight and strategies that you had not considered. Often in these conversations, the best ideas for your next move take shape.

5. **Embrace Discomfort**

Growth requires discomfort. If you are feeling too comfortable, it is time to step into something unfamiliar. Take risks, seek out new opportunities, and push yourself to go beyond what you think you are capable of. The discomfort I felt when stepping into unfamiliar territory is what ultimately pushed me to new heights.

If you are feeling stuck, know that it is not the end – it is just a moment to pause, reflect, and chart a new path forward.

Personal Reflections and Anecdotes on Facing Career Stagnation

The Moment of Realization

Looking back, I can pinpoint the moment I realized something had to change. I was leading a high-profile, global project—the kind of opportunity I used to thrive on. But as the project progressed, something shifted. Instead of feeling energized, I was going through the foggy situation. The work was getting done, but I was not growing. Have you ever felt like that? Like you are moving forward, but not really progressing?

For the first time in my career, I had hit a plateau. I had worked hard, climbed the ladder, earned recognition, and expanded my influence. Yet, there was no excitement, no sense of accomplishment. Success without fulfillment. It was an unsettling realization.

The Crossroads: Comfort vs. Growth

This was not just about the work anymore; it was about my professional identity. I had always defined myself by my achievements, but now I was at a crossroads. Should I continue the familiar, comfortable path? Or should I take a risk and seek something more meaningful?

I am sure many of you have faced a similar choice in your mid-career. It is that moment where you realize that comfort and success do not always equate to growth. I found myself wondering, *What is next? Is this really all there is?*

A Mentor's Perspective: The Vantage Point

During this period, I conversed with one of my mentors, which changed my outlook. I explained how I felt stuck—unsure if I had reached my peak or if there was more, I could achieve. His response was simple but profound: "The plateau is not a dead end. It is a vantage point. From here, you get to decide which mountain to climb next."

That metaphor hit me hard. I was not stuck; I was in a place where I could pause, reflect, and choose my next challenge. It was no longer about waiting for a promotion or hoping for recognition. I needed to take ownership of my growth.

Redefining Success

At this point, I began asking myself difficult questions: *Am I still visible to my leaders? Do they see my potential for new opportunities? Am I pushing myself out of my comfort zone, or have I become complacent?*

These questions were not easy to confront, but they were necessary. I realized I was not being considered for new opportunities because I was not actively seeking them. I had not outgrown my current role—I had just stopped growing within it.

Breaking the Cycle

For many mid-career professionals, this period of reflection can feel daunting. The answer, I found, was in redefining success on my own terms. I had always equated success with external markers—titles, promotions, and recognition.

But now, success had to be measured by something more personal: learning, growth, and the impact I could make on others.

I began pursuing new learning opportunities, expanding my skill set, and seeking out mentors from different industries for fresh perspectives. It was initially uncomfortable, like stepping into unknown territory, but it was exactly what I needed.

Moving Forward with Intention

In the end, the plateau was not a setback—it was a turning point. It forced me to pause, reflect, and decide how I wanted to move forward. For anyone else feeling stuck, I encourage you to see it the same way. This is not the end of the road; it is an opportunity to redefine your path and reignite your sense of purpose.

What mountains are you going to climb next?

Common Challenges and Fears Faced by Mid-Career Professionals

Navigating the Fear of Irrelevance

Have you ever felt like the world is moving ahead while you are standing still? In the midst of our careers, when we have built a rhythm and gained a certain level of success, it can be terrifying to feel the ground shifting beneath us. The fear of irrelevance—of not keeping up with the rapid evolution of our industries—often looms large at this stage. New technologies, younger colleagues with fresh skills, and evolving market demands can leave us questioning our place.

I remember a moment when I realized I was lagging in areas I once mastered. Colleagues, younger and seemingly more agile, were embracing new tools and methodologies while I was clinging to what had worked in the past. The thought crossed my mind: *Am I becoming obsolete?* It was a hard question to face, but ignoring it only deepened the self-doubt.

But here is the thing: this fear of irrelevance is not a dead end; it is a wake-up call. Instead of letting it paralyze you, view it as an opportunity to reinvest in yourself. Ask yourself: *What skills can I sharpen? What new areas can I explore?* Continuous learning is no longer optional—it is essential. I started seeking out mentors, taking courses, and finding ways to embrace new challenges. And you can too.

Facing the Fear of Change: Leaving Comfort Behind

Let's be honest—change is scary. After years of building stability in your career, the idea of stepping away from the familiar can feel like a massive risk. I remember being in a role that I knew inside and out. I had my routine, my network, my reputation. On paper, everything looked fine. But deep down, I knew I had stopped growing.

Does this sound familiar? It is that uneasy feeling when you know you are coasting. The role you once loved now feels like a comfort zone you have outgrown, but the fear of disrupting your stability holds you back. I stayed in that space longer than I should have, paralyzed by the thought of what change might cost me—financial security, relationships, and even my professional identity.

But here is the truth: staying in your comfort zone will lead to stagnation. Yes, change can be disruptive, but it is often where the most growth happens. Take small steps if the leap feels too big. Start by exploring new responsibilities, initiating projects that stretch your skills, or even discussing potential shifts within your role. Growth lives on the other side of change.

Overcoming the Fear of Failure: Rewriting the Narrative

Failure is the one thing that can stop us dead in our tracks. By mid-career, we have built our reputations and earned the trust of our peers. The idea of failing, of making a mistake now, feels like a risk we cannot afford. I get it. The higher we climb, the harder the fall seems.

For years, the fear of failure kept me from pursuing new opportunities. I was so focused on maintaining the status quo, so afraid of making a misstep, that I stopped challenging myself. But here is the thing about failure—it is inevitable. And it is not the enemy. It is part of the process. The biggest growth moments in my career came not from playing it safe but from taking risks, stumbling, and then learning from those mistakes.

What I have learned and want to share with you is that failure is not the end of the story. It is a chapter in the bigger narrative of your growth. Do not avoid it. Embrace it. It is the discomfort, the mistakes, the risks you take that will propel you to the next level.

Moving Forward: Turning Fears into Catalysts

So, where do we go from here? The fears of irrelevance, change, and failure are real, but they do not have to hold you back. Instead, let them be the spark that reignites your drive. Invest in your learning, step outside your comfort zone, and embrace failure as a stepping stone towards growth.

Mid-career is not a plateau—it is a pivot. It is the moment when you get to redefine success on your terms. So, I ask you: *What will you do with this moment? What fears are you ready to face?* Your best days do not have to be behind you. They can start right now.

Conclusion: Moving Beyond the Plateau

Hitting a mid-career plateau can feel overwhelming like you have lost your way after years of hard work. But here is the thing—it is not a dead end; it is a wake-up call. It is your chance to pause, reassess, and ask yourself, *What do I really want next?* Recognizing those early signs of stagnation is not a defeat; it is an invitation to pivot, stretch, and reignite the fire within you. As Winston Churchill said, "Success is not final, failure is not fatal: it is the courage to continue that counts." Navigating this plateau is about having the courage to step outside your comfort zone and lean into the discomfort of growth.

But let's be honest; knowing what to do next is not always clear. It can be messy, confusing, even frustrating. That is why, in the next chapter, I am going to get personal. I will share my own struggles with career stagnation—the moments of doubt, the questions I asked myself, and the small but significant steps I took to get back on track. These are not just strategies; they are real-life reflections. So, if you are feeling stuck, you are not alone. Together, we'll explore the path forward and what it truly takes to Rise and Lead.

Chapter 2

Embracing Change and Uncertainty

The power of mindset shifts in career transitions.

Turning fear of change into opportunities for career growth.

Personal reflections on embracing change in tech.

**"Life is 10% what happens to you and
90% how you react to it."**

- Charles R. Swindoll

The Power of Mindset Shifts in Career Transitions

- Change, though uncomfortable, is the essence of growth. For mid-career professionals, the path ahead often seems full of uncertainty. You may feel like you have hit a plateau, with promotions or opportunities for advancement slowing down. These moments are pivotal; they push us to make one of two choices—stay in the comfort of the known, or step into the unknown, embrace change, and reinvent ourselves.

- However, the key to navigating such a transition successfully lies in **mindset shifts**. Changing your thoughts about your career and potential transforms fear into opportunity. A growth mindset allows you to see change not as an obstacle, but as a powerful tool for reinvention.

- The truth is that mid-career professionals often possess untapped potential. You have already demonstrated your value and experience in various roles. Now, the challenge is to adapt, evolve, and maximize your influence in ways that align with your future aspirations.

Common question tickle our mind at this stage of career is:

- *How can shifting your mindset from fear to opportunity unlock new doors in your career?*

Here are some strategies

Embracing Change and Reinvention — A Powerful Way to Rise and Lead

"Change is the end result of all true learning."
— Leo Buscaglia

Mid-career often arrives unexpectedly, like a jolt that forces you to confront uncomfortable truths about your growth, purpose, and future. The familiar routines that once comforted you can start to feel like traps, leaving you with a haunting question: "What now?" That moment, when you feel stuck and unsure, is where I found myself—and where many of us find ourselves. The powerful realization that helped me Rise and Lead was understanding that **reinvention** was not just an option but a necessity.

But how do you move forward when fear holds you back? How do you break free from the safety of your current path and rebuild a career that feels meaningful and exciting?

Stepping Out of the Fear Zone

It is okay to feel afraid—let's start there. Fear is often the first companion on the road to reinvention. Fear of failure, fear of irrelevance, fear of making the wrong choice. I remember the exact moment when I asked myself, "What if I fail? What if I'm not good enough for the new role I'm eyeing?" These thoughts paralyzed me, keeping me stuck in a cycle of complacency. And that is the reality for many of us. We are **afraid to step out** of what we know, even when it no longer serves us.

But the moment you accept that fear is a natural part of the process—when you make peace with the discomfort—

you begin to unlock your potential. **Reinvention begins** when you take control of your story, step outside your comfort zone, and push beyond the boundaries you have unknowingly set for yourself.

For me, that moment of clarity came when I stopped focusing on why opportunities were passing me by and asked myself a hard question: "What are my gaps?" I had the experience, I had led teams, and I had solved big problems, but I was not evolving. Instead of waiting for recognition, I had to become my own advocate and position myself for the **next chapter** of my career.

Ask yourself:

What am I missing to get to where I want to be?

What story am I telling myself that is keeping me from growing?

The answers to these questions are the first steps toward reinvention. **Fear will always exist**, but you can learn to move with it rather than let it hold you back.

Seeing Through the Eyes of Leadership

One of the hardest lessons I have learned in this journey is that **what you think is impactful** may not always resonate with those in leadership. As mid-career professionals, many of us have spent years mastering our craft—whether it is managing projects, delivering results, or leading teams. But what you might not see is that **leaders want more** than just execution excellence.

I remember delivering a project on time, under budget, and thinking, "This is it—I'll be promoted for sure." But I was not. That is when I realized something critical: **Leaders want vision**. They want you to connect the dots between your work and the organization's strategic goals. They are looking for someone who can not only execute but think big—about the future of the business and how your work fits into the bigger picture.

Ask yourself:

Am I thinking like a leader?

How does my work contribute to the organization's long-term goals?

Leaders like Satish Dhawan, the former chairman of ISRO, understood this shift early on in their careers. Dhawan was known for his exceptional scientific acumen, but he recognized that technical expertise alone would not be enough to propel ISRO forward. He embraced a broader perspective—one that emphasized strategic vision, nurturing talent, and fostering resilience within his team. His empathetic and values-driven leadership, especially during critical moments like the failure of the first Satellite Launch Vehicle (SLV), became the cornerstone of ISRO's long-term success.

This mindset of always evolving and always learning is the foundation for reinvention.

Building Your Future: What You Need to Do

When you are in the middle of a career plateau, it is easy to feel stuck. But **reinvention starts with taking stock of where**

you are and identifying the gaps that are holding you back. It is not just about waiting for the next opportunity to find you—it is about **actively preparing for it**.

Here are the key areas where I found growth necessary for my next step:

1. **Executive Presence**

    This goes beyond delivering great results. It is about how you communicate, carry yourself in meetings, and interact with senior leaders. **Executive presence** is about commanding respect and authority but with humility and authenticity.

2. **Creating Business Impact**

    It is not enough to focus on your tasks—you need to focus on outcomes that move the needle for the company. Find ways to align your projects with the company's strategic goals. How are you contributing to profitability, growth, or efficiency?

3. **Visibility and Networking**

    Do not just do great work—make sure people know about it. Build relationships with senior leaders and **key stakeholders**. Proactively contribute to high-visibility initiatives that align with the business's strategic goals.

4. **Strategic Thinking**

    As you move up, you must shift from focusing on day-to-day tasks to thinking about the **bigger picture**. How does your work contribute to the company's long-term strategy? How can you anticipate challenges and create solutions that will have a lasting impact?

5. **Continuous Learning**

   The learning journey does not end in mid-career. In fact, this is the time when it becomes even more critical. The most successful leaders are those who are always learning—whether it is new skills, new technologies, or new ways of thinking.

The Importance of Building Your Network

Networking is not just about connections—it is about building **meaningful relationships** with people who can support your growth. Early in my career, I thought networking was about attending events and exchanging business cards. But real networking is about sharing ideas, offering help, and creating value for others. When I started networking with purpose, I realized how powerful it could be for my growth.

Proactively build relationships with people in leadership, share your ideas, and offer to collaborate on initiatives that matter. Leaders appreciate professionals who bring **new perspectives** to the table—people who are unafraid to offer bold solutions.

Setting Career Goals: Short and Long-Term

The final step in reinvention is setting clear, **intentional career goals**. What do you want your career to look like in the next 5 or 10 years? Without a vision, it is easy to drift. But with a clear sense of where you want to go, you can take specific actions to get there.

What are your **short-term goals**? What skills do you need to build, and what relationships do you need to strengthen?

What are your **long-term goals**? How do you want to be remembered as a leader, and what kind of impact do you want to have?

By setting intentional goals and focusing on continuous growth, you can **Rise and Lead** from any mid-career plateau.

Overcoming Fear: The First Step to Reinvention

Mid-career can feel like a balancing act—between what you have built and the unknown future. At this stage, fear of failure often becomes the biggest obstacle. You have spent years crafting a reputation and reaching a certain level of success. The idea of starting over, of possibly failing, can feel paralyzing. But here is something to remember failure is not the end—it is part of the learning process.

Think about the leaders you admire. Satya Nadella did not just become CEO of Microsoft by sticking to what he knew. He pushed beyond his technical expertise, reinventing himself to focus on strategic thinking, empathy, and business growth. Jeff Bezos had colossal failures at Amazon—the Fire Phone, for example. Yet each misstep became a stepping stone toward success because he embraced the lessons from those failures.

What about you? Are you letting the fear of failure hold you back? What if failure was part of your growth? The most powerful shift happens when you begin to see failure as a necessary part of success. It is not about whether you will stumble but how you rise again, using the lessons learned.

Reinventing Yourself: What is Next?

The process of reinventing yourself is not just about learning new skills or gaining promotions—it is about shifting your mindset. You are not defined by your past successes or setbacks. Reinvention is a choice, one you can make today by stepping into the unknown and allowing yourself to grow through the experience.

This journey requires a new perspective: think like a leader, align your contributions with larger organizational goals, and step out of your comfort zone. Where are your gaps? How can you learn what is necessary to not just keep up, but excel?

Your Story, Your Rise

Imagine this moment as your turning point. What do you want the next chapter of your career to look like? The opportunities ahead are vast, but the question is, will you take the leap? Will you rise again, stronger and more resilient, ready to create the impact you have always aspired to?

Now it is your turn. What will you do today to embrace change and take the first step toward reinvention?

Embracing Change: A Personal Journey in the Tech World

"Change is the only constant."

This phrase may seems odd, but in the tech industry, it rings true. Technologies evolve, roles shift, and organizations restructure constantly. For mid-career professionals, the fear of change can feel overwhelming, but it is also the gateway to growth.

As someone who has navigated the spectrum from Individual Contributor (IC) to People Manager and back again, I have learned that embracing change is not just about survival—it is about thriving. In fact, the times I feared change the most were often the times I needed it most. Those moments of uncertainty have forced me to reinvent myself, learn new skills, and build a more holistic career.

Moving Between Roles: IC to People Manager (and Back Again)

When I first transitioned from an IC to a People Manager, I felt like I was thrown into deep waters. My comfort zone was technical expertise—contributing to specific tasks and owning my deliverables. Suddenly, I had to lead others, set a vision for the team, and balance the needs of both individuals and the business. It was daunting. There were days I longed for the simplicity of my IC days, where my personal contributions measured success.

But leadership taught me something invaluable: it is not about what *you* can achieve, but what you can help others achieve. Leading teams challenged me to see the bigger picture and grow my skills in strategic thinking, empathy, and conflict resolution. Each step felt like a reinvention.

That said, the path was not always upward. At times, due to organizational strategic focus, I found myself stepping back into an IC role to lead as Global program manager for critical projects. At first, I feared it was a demotion, a sign of failure. But soon, I realized it was an opportunity to dive deeper into my technical and program management skills being onsite (US location) and gain a renewed perspective on leadership from the ground up. Moving between these roles was not a setback—it was a way to become more versatile and adaptable. In fact, the strategic IC role helped to polish my skills in adaptability, Strategic focus, and global connect. The benefit was – I effectively played a transition leader role when a couple of sites had to close. The outcome was the successful transition of projects to the HGR site, and huge savings on cost.

Many mid-career professionals see moving between IC and managerial roles as a loss of status. But from my experience, each role has enriched the other. Managing teams has made me a better individual contributor, and my IC work has made me a more empathetic leader.

Reflection Questions:

How have role transitions shaped your understanding of your career?

Are you open to moving between IC and leadership roles to grow your skill set?

Learning from Leaders: Satya Nadella's Journey of Reinvention

Look at Satya Nadella's career. Before he became Microsoft's CEO, he moved between various roles in engineering, product development, and cloud computing. His adaptability in navigating these transitions prepared him to lead one of the world's most transformative tech companies. When Nadella took over, Microsoft was not the dominant software giant it had once been. Instead of fearing the change, he leaned into it—transforming the company into a leader in cloud computing and artificial intelligence.

Nadella's story teaches us that the key to growth lies in leveraging transitions. It is not about avoiding change but embracing it as a catalyst for reinvention. The same is true for us. No matter where we are in our careers, transitions—whether they are role changes or new organizational directions—offer us the chance to grow, learn, and lead.

Navigating Organizational Changes: Embracing the People Factor

"Change is never just about the role—it's about the people we work with and the bonds we build. Over the years, I have had the privilege of working alongside incredibly talented individuals, some of whom had to move on due to organizational restructuring or site closures. These moments are undeniably tough—watching impactful colleagues leave is never easy. I still recall a significant restructuring within a Center of Excellence (CoE) structure I was part of. It led to many valued team members moving on, and their absence was deeply felt. Yet, these experiences taught me the importance of adaptability, resilience, and valuing the contributions of every individual."

I remember working with a vendor to offload routine tasks so my team could focus on innovation. Initially, it felt like giving up control, but in reality, it freed us to tackle more meaningful challenges. This experience reinforced a critical leadership lesson—delegation and trust are essential for growth.

Reflection Questions:

Have you experienced organizational changes that forced you to rethink your role or leadership approach?

How did you turn those moments into opportunities for growth?

Tim Cook's Leadership Transition: Leading with Vision

Tim Cook faced one of the most challenging transitions in the tech world when he took over from Steve Jobs at Apple. Many doubted whether Cook could lead Apple with the same innovation. Instead of trying to be another Steve Jobs, Cook embraced his own leadership style. He expanded Apple into new markets like wearables and services, focusing on operational excellence while maintaining the company's innovative edge.

Cook's journey is a reminder that successful leadership is not about replicating the past—it is about honoring it while forging a new path forward. Whether you are stepping into a new role or facing organizational shifts, remember that change is not something to fear—it is an opportunity to lead with vision.

Your Turn: What Will You Do?

Now it is your turn to reflect. How will you embrace change and reinvention in your own career? Will you step into the unknown, confident that every transition—whether IC to the manager or navigating a company shift—holds the potential for growth?

Your next chapter is waiting. What will you do today to make it happen?

Conclusion: Growth Through Change

For mid-career professionals, change can often feel like a breaking point. But in reality, it is a turning point – a powerful catalyst for growth. Whether you are shifting from an individual contributor to a People Manager, facing organizational restructuring, or navigating personal uncertainties, every transition is an opportunity to redefine yourself.

I have lived this truth. There were times when the fear of stepping into the unknown almost paralyzed me. But with every role shift, every reorganization, I learned that change does not diminish you—it expands you. It pushes you to develop new skills, gain deeper insights, and build resilience.

In tech, where innovation is relentless, staying adaptable is not just a survival strategy—it is the key to thriving.

Think about your own career. What if the changes you face are not obstacles but opportunities for reinvention? How could embracing them unlock the next level of your growth?

Growth comes not from staying where you are comfortable but from daring to step into the unknown. As you reflect on the changes in your own career, consider what lies beyond the discomfort. How will you use these experiences to fuel your next chapter?

Final Reflection Question: How can you shift your mindset to see change as the path to new possibilities in your career?

In the next chapter, we'll explore how to *define your career direction* amid the uncertainty of change and how to chart a path that aligns with your personal and professional goals. Change is inevitable, but the clarity you bring to it defines your future. Let's take the next step.

The bottom line is this: You are capable of more than you know. The discomfort you feel right now is a sign that it is time to step into a new version of yourself. Embrace the change. **Reinvent yourself. Rise and Lead.**

Part 2

Defining Your Career Direction

Chapter 3

Defining Your Vision, Mission, and Goals

The significance of having clarity and purpose in your career

How to create a powerful vision and set strategic goals.

Aligning personal and professional objectives for lasting success.

> "Take up one idea. Make that one idea your
> life – think of it, dream of it, and live on
> that idea. Let the brain, muscles, nerves, every part
> of your body, be full of that idea, and just leave every
> other idea alone. This is the way to success".
> – Swami Vivekananda

Crafting Clarity: A Guide for Mid-Career Professionals

Imagine setting out on a road trip without knowing where you are headed. You might enjoy the scenery for a while, but soon, you will start feeling lost, unsure of the destination, and anxious about wasting time. Now, think about your career. Are you driving toward a destination or just coasting along? Many mid-career professionals reach a point where they realize they have been on autopilot, moving from one job to another without a clear sense of purpose. That is when the frustration creeps in, and suddenly, you are facing a mid-career crisis.

But here is the thing: You are not alone. And the good news is that you can take control.

In this chapter, we'll dive into why clarity in your career is the compass that will guide you forward. We'll explore how to create a career vision that excites and challenges you and how to break that vision into actionable, strategic goals that lead to real change. Together, we'll reshape how you see your future, so instead of feeling stuck, you will be empowered to take the driver's seat.

The Importance of Clarity: The Right Compass for Career Growth

I want to share a story with you about my friend Sam (name changed). Sam is brilliant—an expert in his field with 15 years of experience—but he felt like he was just spinning his wheels.

He worked hard and delivered results, but as the years passed, his work felt routine. Sam confessed that he no longer knew what he wanted in his career. "What's the point?" he asked me. I'm just moving from project to project."

Many mid-career professionals experience this sense of drifting. Like Sam, you might feel like you are doing everything right but still are not sure where it is all leading. You get caught up in the daily grind—deadlines, meetings, tactical tasks—and lose sight of the bigger picture.

But here is the truth: Clarity is the key to turning this around. Without clarity, we make decisions reactively. But when we know what we want, every step we take brings us closer to that goal.

> "The most important decision you make is to
> be in a good mood."
> –Voltaire

The moment Sam sat down and took the time to articulate his vision for the future, everything changed. He had a clear direction for where he wanted to go. Clarity is not just about knowing your next job—it is about understanding how all the pieces of your career align with your long-term goals. It gives you purpose. It fuels your motivation when things get tough.

So, let me ask you: **Do you know where you want to go?**

Take a moment. Reflect. What do you want your career to look like in 5 or 10 years? What excites you? What impact do you want to have?

Crafting a Vision: Building the Blueprint for Long-Term Success

One of the most powerful things you can do for yourself is create a compelling vision for your career. It is more than a list of goals—it is about painting a picture of what your future looks like and how it aligns with your personal values and aspirations. You can use visualization techniques to come up with your vision and long term goals.

I once worked with a colleague, Maya, who had reached a leadership role in her company but felt restless. She had achieved what she thought she wanted, yet something was missing. It was not until she took the time to reflect on the big questions that her path became clear:

What kind of impact do I want to make?

How do I want to be remembered professionally?

What problems am I passionate about solving?

Maya realized that while she was successful, her true passion was in mentorship and developing future leaders, something her current role did not allow her to fully embrace. This realization led her to pivot and create a vision centered around leadership development, eventually leading her to a fulfilling career as an executive coach.

Your vision does not need to be grand like Elon Musk's goal of colonizing Mars, but it does need to be yours. It needs to resonate deeply with you, providing you with the "why" that drives you forward every day.

Now, think about your own career: **What kind of legacy do you want to leave?**

When you have clarity about your vision, you have something to refer to whenever you make career decisions. Like Maya, you will have a North Star that keeps you aligned and focused on what truly matters.

Setting Strategic Goals: Transforming Your Vision into Action

Once you have defined your vision, the next step is to break it down into actionable goals. This is where the rubber meets the road. Too often, mid-career professionals have a vision but fail to translate it into concrete steps they can take. The result? Stagnation.

Let's revisit Sam's story. Once he had his vision in place—becoming a thought leader in his industry—he felt energized. But his next hurdle was figuring out **how** to get there. We sat down and mapped out two types of goals:

1. **Short-term goals**: Things Sam could accomplish in the next 6 to 12 months, such as leading a cross-functional project and starting to publish industry insights online.

2. **Long-term goals**: His broader ambitions over the next 5 to 10 years, like becoming a speaker at industry conferences and transitioning into a more strategic role.

Breaking your vision into short- and long-term goals allows you to see progress. Each goal becomes a stepping stone toward your larger vision.

Now, let's think about you. If your long-term goal is to become a leader in your field, what short-term steps can you take? Maybe it is leading a new initiative at work, networking with key people in your industry, or gaining a certification that aligns with your career path.

The key is to keep moving. The worst thing you can do is stand still. With every small action you take, you are building momentum, even if it does not feel like it at the time.

Turning Setbacks into Stepping Stones

Here is the part no one likes to talk about: You are going to face setbacks. It is inevitable. But clarity and goal setting give you the resilience to turn those setbacks into stepping stones.

Oprah Winfrey is a prime example. Most people know her as a media mogul, but what is often overlooked is the clarity and persistence that got her there. Early in her career, she faced rejection and failure, but she always had a vision of building a media empire that empowered and inspired millions. Every step she took was intentional, from launching 'The Oprah Winfrey Show' to creating 'OWN', her own network.

When challenges come your way, having a clear vision and actionable goals gives you the resilience to push through. Each setback becomes a lesson, a necessary detour on your path to success.

Final Thoughts: Reclaim Your Career

If you are feeling lost or stuck in your career, know that you have the power to change that narrative. Start by clarifying what you want—do not wait for life to happen to you. Craft a vision that excites and motivates you, and then break it down into manageable steps. It is time to take control of your career and steer it in the direction you want to go.

Remember, as Tony Robbins says: **"Setting goals is the first step in turning the invisible into the visible."**

Your career is not just a series of random events; it is a journey. You have the map in your hands, and now it is up to you to follow it.

"Arise, awake, and stop not till the goal is reached."
- by Swami Vivekananda

This timeless message inspired me countless times to take action with determination and perseverance, emphasizing the importance of staying focused and resolute in achieving goals.

Reflection Questions:

What does your vision for the next 5-10 years look like?

Are your current actions aligned with that vision?

What steps can you take today to move closer to your ultimate career destination?

____

____

____

____

____

____

____

____

____

Up Next: Aligning Personal and Professional Objectives for Lasting Success

Now that you have crafted your vision and set strategic goals, it is time to ensure that your personal values and professional ambitions are in harmony. In the next topic, we'll explore how to align these two areas to create a fulfilling and balanced career. Because true success is not just about professional achievement—it is about finding a sense of purpose that resonates across all areas of your life.

Aligning Personal and Professional Objectives for Lasting Success

The Power of Alignment in Career Success

Imagine this: You are standing at a crossroads in your mid-career. You have accomplished a lot professionally, built a solid reputation, and maybe even earned the promotions you once dreamed of. But despite your external success, something inside feels unsettled. The career that once energized you now leaves you feeling drained. Your personal life has taken a back seat, and you wonder if you are still heading in the right direction. Sound familiar?

This is a pivotal moment many mid-career professionals face—a time to recalibrate and ask, "What do I truly want?" It is time to align your personal and professional objectives, not just for career success but for lasting fulfillment.

Why Alignment Matters

As you progress through your career, success is not just about climbing the corporate ladder anymore. It is about balancing work demands with personal aspirations, family commitments, and self-care. When there's alignment between your career and the life you want to live, it creates a sense of purpose and clarity. But when these two worlds are out of sync, the result can be burnout, stress, and a deep sense of dissatisfaction.

I have seen this struggle firsthand. A colleague of mine, let's call him Ravi, was a high-achieving director in his company, managing large teams and delivering results that made waves. On paper, everything was perfect. But outside of work, he felt disconnected—from his family, his hobbies, and even himself. It was not until he took a step back, reevaluated his priorities, and aligned his personal goals with his professional ambitions that he found his true sense of fulfillment.

Balance vs. Alignment

Let's talk about the difference between balance and alignment. We often hear about "work-life balance," but in reality, it is more like a juggling act—trying to split time evenly between everything. But is that realistic? Not really. True fulfillment comes from alignment, not balance. Alignment means structuring your career and life so that they support each other rather than compete for your time and energy.

Think of it as a puzzle. Each piece—your career, family, health, and personal interests—needs to fit together. When they do, the picture becomes clearer. It is not about giving each piece equal time but ensuring they connect in a way that feels right for you.

Why Mid-Career is the Ideal Time to Align

Why does this inner tug-of-war happen during mid-career? Often, it is because we are at a stage of life where we have more responsibilities—whether it is family, finances, or health. The unrelenting drive for professional success that once motivated you might now feel at odds with these personal demands.

Take a moment to reflect: Have you felt torn between pushing for that next promotion and spending quality time with your loved ones? Or maybe, like Ravi, you have achieved career milestones but lost sight of the things that once brought you joy. This is the ideal time to reassess, realign, and redefine success on your own terms.

Reflection Time:

Are you satisfied with how your career supports your personal life?

Have certain aspects of your personal life suffered because of professional ambitions?

Aligning Your Objectives: Strategies for Lasting Success

Aligning your personal and professional goals is not something that happens overnight. It requires deep reflection, intentional decisions, and a willingness to adjust. Here are a few steps to help guide you through this process.

1. Clarify Your Personal Values

    What truly matters to you? Take a moment to think about your core values. These are the principles that guide your decisions and shape your vision for life. Is family a priority? Do you value health and well-being? Maybe creativity or giving back to your community is important to you.

    In the rush of everyday life, it is easy to lose sight of these values. But when you take the time to clarify them, you gain a clearer sense of what you want out of both your personal life and your career. For example, Satish Dhawan, the former chairman of ISRO, demonstrated the power of aligning personal values with professional excellence. Despite the failure of India's first Satellite Launch Vehicle (SLV), Dhawan took full responsibility as a leader, shielding his team from blame. This act of humility and accountability became a turning point for ISRO, fostering a culture of resilience and trust that ultimately led to the organization's groundbreaking successes. His leadership serves as a timeless lesson on the importance of empathy and values-driven decisions in achieving long-term growth.

Reflection: Write down three values that are most important to you right now. Do your current professional goals align with these values?

2. Create Overlapping Goals

One of the best ways to align your personal and professional objectives is to create goals that serve both areas. For instance, if you are passionate about health, integrate fitness into your workday by taking walking meetings or scheduling breaks for exercise. If spending more time with family is a priority, look for flexible work arrangements or remote opportunities.

The key here is to stop viewing your personal and professional life as two separate entities. Instead, think of them as complementary. When you find opportunities to overlap, you will create a sense of harmony that brings more energy and fulfillment into both areas.

Reflection: Think about one personal goal you have. How can you align it with your career? Write down one action you can take this week to make it happen.

3. Set Boundaries and Communicate Clearly

    Setting boundaries is critical, especially in mid-career, when professional demands can easily spill into personal time. It is important to be intentional about where you draw the line. Are there certain hours you want to dedicate to family? Are there times when you need space for personal reflection or hobbies? Be clear with yourself and your employer about these boundaries.

    Sheryl Sandberg, former COO of Facebook, experienced a life-changing event when she lost her husband. In the aftermath, she became a strong advocate for flexible work policies, understanding firsthand the importance of balancing personal and professional needs. Her decision to set boundaries allowed her to remain effective at work while also prioritizing her personal life.

    Reflection: What boundaries can you set to ensure that your personal life isn't overshadowed by work? How can you communicate these boundaries clearly to others?

4. Take Inventory and Refocus Your Priorities

    Sometimes, the first step to aligning personal and professional goals is simply becoming aware of where they currently stand. Take a moment to write down both your personal and professional goals side by side. Are they aligned? Do they complement each other? Or do you see a conflict between the two?

If you notice areas of misalignment, ask yourself what needs to change. Is it your professional focus? Are you dedicating too much energy to certain projects at the expense of your health or family? Refocus your priorities so that you can create a career and life that support each other.

Reflection: Take five minutes to list your current goals. Do they reflect your true priorities? What needs to change to bring them into alignment?

Richard Branson, founder of the Virgin Group, is a notable example of aligning personal and professional objectives. Branson has consistently emphasized the importance of work-life balance, often sharing how he prioritizes time with his family and personal adventures alongside his business ventures. By creating a company culture that values flexibility and personal fulfillment, Branson aligned his entrepreneurial pursuits with his passion for travel and adventure. His ability to blend personal interests with professional goals helped him build a thriving global business without sacrificing his personal happiness or relationships.

Moving Forward: The Lasting Impact of Alignment

As you move forward in your career, remember that true success is not just about professional accolades or financial gains. It is about creating a life that feels meaningful and fulfilling. When your personal and professional objectives are aligned, you are not only more likely to achieve career success, but you will do so in a way that enriches your life outside of work.

In the next chapter, we'll dive deeper into actionable steps you can take to align your personal and professional objectives for lasting success. You will learn how to create personal branding, and take practical steps to gain visibility in your company or industry.

Final Reflection:

Are there areas in your professional life that conflict with your personal goals?

What steps can you take today to bring more harmony between your work and personal life?

Chapter 4

Personal Branding and Visibility

Building a personal brand that differentiates you in the IT industry.

Gaining visibility and influence with decision-makers.

Strategies for increasing your visibility within your company and in the industry.

> "Your brand is what people say about you when
> you're not in the room."
> — Jeff Bezos

Why Personal Branding is Key to Thriving in the IT Industry

In the world of IT, where change happens faster than we can blink, it is easy to get lost in the shuffle. Many of us, particularly as mid-career professionals, have spent years putting our heads down, grinding away, and thinking that hard work alone will speak for itself. I have been there—believing that technical skills, dedication, and late nights would eventually lead to the recognition I deserved. But let me ask you something: How many times have you been passed over for an opportunity, a promotion, or even a "thank you" after all your effort?

The truth is hard work alone is not enough. Not anymore. If people don't know what you bring to the table, how can they value it?

This is where personal branding steps in. It is not about self-promotion or ego; it is about **making sure the right people see the value you bring**. Personal branding is your way of standing out—not just as another tech professional with certifications and skills, but as a unique individual who offers something no one else can.

My Wake-Up Call: Why Personal Branding Matters

I used to think that as long as I performed well, everything else would fall into place. Year after year, I trusted my career growth to my manager, believing they knew my worth. I figured, "They see my hard work, they'll reward me." But guess what? The opportunities I longed for never came my way.

One day, after being passed over *yet again*, I realized something: It was not about whether I was capable. It was that no one *knew* I was capable. I had spent so much time focusing on the work that I forgot to focus on showing my worth to others. And so, I began to shift my thinking. I did not need to be the loudest in the room, but I needed to make sure my contributions were not invisible.

Can you relate? It is not about being better than others—it is about making sure *your* unique value is seen and understood by the right people.

What Makes You Different?

Now, let's think about you for a second. What makes *you* stand out? In a sea of IT professionals, all armed with technical skills, certifications, and experience, what differentiates you?

It is not just about what you do—it is about *how* you do it. Here are a few questions to ask yourself:

What is your niche? Maybe you are an expert in cloud transitions, or maybe you have led high-performing Agile teams. Figure out your specialty and own it.

How do you lead? People do not just remember what you know—they remember how you made them feel, how you supported them, and how you inspired them.

What values drive you? Authenticity, integrity, and consistency matter more than you think. Your values shape your brand just as much as your technical abilities.

For me, my turning point was identifying my differentiator—Strategic Focus, Innovative business model to increase the revenues, and **tackling product continuity for revenue flow in the high-tech industry**. That became my brand, my value-add. Suddenly, I was not just another IT professional—I was someone with a unique skill set that could solve real problems.

Building Your Personal Brand: Where to Start

Building your personal brand is not something that happens overnight. It is a journey that requires reflection, action, and evolution. But here is how you can get started:

1. Define Your Brand

    Start by answering these questions:

    What are my core strengths?

    What unique value do I bring to my teams and projects?

    How do I want to be remembered after people work with me?

    This will help you write down a concise **brand statement**—your personal pitch that reflects who you are and what you bring to the table. This becomes your compass in building your personal brand.

2. Build Your Digital Presence

    In today's world, if you are not visible online, you are invisible. LinkedIn is your stage—make it work for you. Share your insights, comment on industry trends, publish articles, and build your network. I started by posting videos about goal setting and visualization techniques. The response was overwhelming. Suddenly, I was not just another professional—I was a thought leader.

    Remember, people do not know what you bring to the table unless you show them.

3. Network with Purpose

    Networking is not just about attending conferences or collecting LinkedIn connections—it is about *building relationships*. Engage with people authentically. Offer your help, share your knowledge, and be a connector. Your brand grows every time someone associates you with value.

4. Stay Curious and Keep Learning

    Your personal brand should evolve just as the IT industry evolves. Do not get stuck in one place. Keep learning, keep growing, and keep sharing what you learn with others. It is what will keep your brand relevant.

Your Brand: A Bridge to Gaining Visibility and Influence

Building a personal brand is a lot like building a bridge between where you are now and where you want to go. Your brand is what makes you memorable in the right circles and helps you gain visibility with decision-makers who can elevate your career.

This journey does not stop here. In the next section, we'll explore a critical aspect of personal branding: Gaining Visibility and Influence with Decision-Makers. This is where the real magic happens—when you are not just seen but heard by those who can most impact your career.

Let's cross that bridge together.

Building Visibility and Influence with Key Decision-Makers

Why Mid-Career Visibility Can Unlock Your Growth

You have consistently delivered—project after project, meeting every deadline, exceeding expectations. Yet, despite your hard work and dedication, you feel overlooked. Promotions bypass you, your contributions go unnoticed, and the leadership roles you dream of seem just beyond your reach. Gaining visibility and influence with decision-makers is the missing link to ensure your efforts are recognized and rewarded.

Does this sound familiar? If so, you are not alone.

Mid-career is a tricky phase. The expectations are higher, and the rules of the game have shifted. It is no longer just about doing great work. It is about making sure the right people *see* your great work. In this stage of your career, visibility becomes your ticket to growth. But here is the catch: if decision-makers—your boss, senior leadership, key stakeholders—are unaware of your contributions, you risk being overlooked, no matter how exceptional you are.

I get it. Early in my career, I had the same mindset. I assumed that hard work would speak for itself. I kept my head down, delivered results, and trusted that, eventually, I would be noticed. But I was not. After hitting that invisible ceiling, I confronted a hard truth: *great work without visibility is like performing on a stage with no audience.* The applause and recognition come when the right people see you. It was a difficult lesson to learn, but once I did, everything changed.

Visibility is not about self-promotion or ego. It is about ensuring decision-makers—those who hold the keys to your next big opportunity—understand your value. When you are visible, they not only recognize your work, but they also start looking to you for leadership, strategy, and influence.

Understanding What Decision-Makers Value

Before we dive into how to get noticed, let's take a step back. It is not enough to be seen—you must be seen for the *right* things. Decision-makers care less about the tasks you are ticking off your to-do list and more about the outcomes you drive.

They ask themselves: *What results is this person delivering?* It is not just about completing a project—it is about how that project impacts the organization. Are you saving the company time, money, or resources? Are you pushing the needle forward in a meaningful way?

Here is where the shift happens. When I stopped focusing on the minutiae of my daily tasks and started communicating the impact of my work—how I contributed to strategic goals, how I improved efficiency, and how my leadership drove tangible results—decision-makers started to notice.

Think about it. In your own work, how are you making a difference? What would happen if you framed your contributions in terms of results rather than tasks? The people in power want to know how you influence the bigger picture. If you can connect your work to organizational success, you have already taken a significant step toward gaining their attention.

A Personal Reflection: The Turning Point

I remember a pivotal moment in my own journey. There was a project outside of my usual scope of work—something that was not initially my responsibility but aligned with my interests. I could have stayed in my lane, continued doing what I was already good at, and hoped for recognition down the road. But instead, I stepped up. I volunteered to lead the initiative, knowing it would allow me to work directly with senior leaders who had not previously been aware of my contributions.

That decision changed everything. Not only did I build a relationship with an influential executive, but my work was suddenly on their radar. They could see the impact I was making, and doors that once felt locked began to open.

That is the power of being visible—not just in your department but across the organization.

Engage: Take a Moment to Reflect

Now, pause for a second. Think about your own career. Can you recall a time when you felt overlooked despite your hard work? What would it look like for you to take a more proactive role in gaining visibility? How could you communicate your results in a way that resonates with decision-makers? Jot down one or two recent accomplishments and consider how they contributed to the company's success.

Connection to the Next Step: Strategies for Gaining Visibility

Visibility does not happen by accident; it is a conscious, ongoing effort. In the next section, we'll dig into specific strategies you can start using today to increase your visibility within your company and across the industry. We'll explore practical steps like how to build relationships with key decision-makers, how to communicate your wins without sounding boastful, and how to ensure your work is not just being done—it is being noticed.

Remember: being great at your job is essential, but being seen as great is what propels you forward.

Let's dive in.

Strategies for Increasing Your Visibility Within Your Company and in the Industry

The Importance of Visibility in Advancing Your Career

In today's fast-paced IT world, simply doing your job well is insufficient to move you up the ladder. You can deliver flawless results, log extra hours, and be the best at what you do—but still be overlooked for promotions or leadership roles. Why? Because no one sees you. Many mid-career professionals, despite years of experience, fall into the trap of thinking hard work will speak for itself. I have been there too, waiting for the day someone would recognize my dedication and results.

It took me a while to realize that visibility is crucial. Being good at your job is not enough. You need to make sure others know your strengths, values, and the unique contribution you bring to the table. If key decision-makers do not see you, you will continue to feel invisible, wondering why your career is stuck. This chapter is not about bragging or being someone you are not. It is about being visible in an authentic way—inside your organization and within your industry.

Personal Reflection

In the earlier part of my career, I assumed that if I worked hard enough, promotions would naturally follow. But the reality was very different. I watched others move up the ranks while I stayed in place, frustrated and unsure of what I was doing wrong. One day, a mentor asked me a simple but powerful question: *"Does your boss even know what you're doing or what you are creating?"* That moment shifted everything for me. I began to focus on not just doing good work but making sure the right people knew about it. And that is when the opportunities started coming.

Strategy 1: Seek Out High-Visibility Projects

It is easy to stay in your comfort zone and stick to the tasks assigned to you, but if you want to stand out, you must proactively seek out projects that matter. These are the projects that senior leadership cares about—the ones tied to the company's goals. Volunteering for such initiatives gives you a chance to showcase your abilities to those who have the power to move your career forward.

For instance, a colleague of mine noticed our company was struggling with rolling out a new system. It was not her responsibility, but she offered to lead the transition. This move put her in direct contact with senior leaders, and soon after, she was promoted. What are the projects in your company that no one else is stepping up for? Could you be the one to take the lead?

Strategy 2: Speak Up in Meetings

I get it—speaking up in meetings can feel intimidating, especially when senior people are in the room. But staying silent does not serve you or your career. When you contribute your insights or ask thoughtful questions, you remind people of your expertise. It can be as simple as offering a solution to a challenge everyone discusses. Decision-makers notice those who consistently bring value to the table.

Think back to a recent meeting where you had something to say but did not. How could that moment have been an opportunity for visibility? Imagine how different things could be if, in your next meeting, you share your thoughts. Try it. You might be surprised by the impact it has.

Strategy 3: Build Relationships with Decision-Makers

Visibility is not just about being seen; it is about being known—by the right people. Building genuine relationships with influencers, mentors, and decision-makers within your company is key to advancing your career. Early on, I made the mistake of focusing only on my work and neglecting relationships. But when I started networking across teams, I realized that people did not just know me for my skills but for my character and insights. Those relationships opened doors that hard work alone could not.

Who are the key people in your organization? How well do they know you? Take the time to connect with them, even if it feels out of your comfort zone.

Visibility Beyond Your Company

Your career growth is not limited to what happens within the walls of your office. In today's digital age, your visibility within the broader industry can also play a critical role. Establishing yourself as a thought leader through social media, online articles, and industry conferences can position you as someone with expertise and influence.

I had a colleague who felt stuck in her job. She began posting her insights on LinkedIn, and within months, she was being approached for speaking engagements and eventually earned a more visible role within her company. How could you take one step today towards sharing your knowledge with the wider world?

Conclusion: Build Visibility to Build Opportunities

It is time to stop waiting for someone to notice your hard work and start taking control of your visibility. The more people see you and understand your value, the more doors will open for you. But remember, visibility without value is just noise. Your goal is to consistently show up and deliver value—whether inside your company or within the industry. When you do that, opportunities will come.

As you grow in visibility, you will find yourself stepping into leadership roles, whether it is leading a project or managing a team. The next chapter will dive into what it takes to transition into leadership and manage teams effectively. How do you lead with authenticity, inspire your team, and continue building on the visibility you have earned? Let's explore that next.

Part 3

Building Leadership and Managing Teams

Chapter 5

Developing Leadership Traits and Managing Teams

Key leadership traits every IT professional should master.

Transitioning from an individual contributor to a leader.

Key Leadership Traits Every IT Professional Should Master

Leadership in the IT industry goes far beyond technical proficiency. While deep technological understanding is crucial, it is the human-centered leadership traits that truly elevate successful professionals, particularly for those in mid-career who are striving to break through the plateau. As an IT professional, you are already familiar with how fast technology changes. What is often harder to grasp is that your leadership skills must evolve just as rapidly to keep pace—not just with tech, but with the people you lead. The ability to inspire, guide, and support a team while aligning with the company's broader vision is what will ultimately define the legacy you leave behind.

In my own journey, there came a time when my technical skills alone were no longer enough. I realized I had to shift my focus from solving problems with my hands to solving them with my head and heart. I was not just writing code anymore; I was influencing decisions, rallying teams, and managing expectations—all while navigating the fast-paced tech world. This realization became the turning point in my career, and I want to share the lessons I learned along the way to help you thrive as a leader in this industry.

1. Emotional Intelligence: The Heartbeat of Leadership

    When I first heard about emotional intelligence (EI), I brushed it off as something for the HR department to worry about. However, I quickly learned that no technical expertise could replace the importance of empathy and emotional awareness in leadership. During a particularly stressful project—one with tight deadlines, frequent scope changes, and a geographically dispersed team—I saw firsthand how emotions could either break a team apart or pull it together.

One of my team members, Ram (name changed), was struggling. His performance was slipping, but instead of asking for help, he grew more isolated. The younger me might have just pushed harder, assuming he needed a shove. But by engaging with Ram one-on-one, I discovered he was dealing with personal issues that were spilling into his work. A simple conversation, where I acknowledged his emotions, made all the difference. It was not about solving his problems but about showing that I cared. Once we addressed his emotional needs, his productivity improved, and the team's overall morale lifted.

In an industry like IT, where stress levels can soar, and projects can feel like sprints in a marathon, emotional intelligence is the secret weapon. Understanding both your emotions and those of your team is what will separate you from a manager and turn you into a leader.

Ask yourself: When was the last time I asked my team members how they felt, not just about the work, but about life? How can I create a space where they feel comfortable sharing?

2. Visionary Thinking: From Manager to Leader

Leadership in IT also means being able to anticipate and plan for the future. It is easy to get caught up in the immediate issues—bug fixes, sprints, deadlines—but true leaders are always scanning the horizon. I remember a time when our organization was considering adopting cloud technologies long before they became standard. While many of my peers were content with the status quo, I saw where the industry was headed and began preparing my team for this shift. We did not wait until we were forced to adopt cloud computing; we led the charge. That forward-thinking mindset sets us apart.

Think about it: What trends are on the horizon that might impact your team or your organization? How can you prepare them for future challenges and opportunities?

Leading with vision also means having a clear picture of where you want your team to go—and then inspiring them to get there. It is not just about the end goal but how you communicate that vision. People need to believe in what they are working toward. Steve Jobs was known for his visionary thinking, but his genius was not just in imagining products like the iPhone—it was in convincing others that it could be done, even when it seemed impossible.

Ask yourself: How can I communicate my vision in a way that excites and motivates my team?

3. Adaptability: Leading in a World of Constant Change

   The IT world is nothing if not unpredictable. New technologies emerge almost overnight, customer demands shift, and business strategies evolve. As a leader, you must be adaptable, not just for yourself but for your team. When I transitioned from an individual contributor role to leading my first team, I thought I had everything figured out. But nothing prepares you for the curveballs that leadership throws at you.

   I recall a project where we were halfway through the development cycle when the client abruptly changed the project's scope. It happens to many of us right? My initial reaction was frustration—months of planning seemed wasted. But instead of letting that frustration show, I pivoted. I brought the team together and framed the situation as an opportunity to challenge ourselves. By leading with flexibility, we not only delivered on time but exceeded the client's expectations.

   Reflect: How do I handle sudden changes? Do I communicate adaptability and resilience to my team?

4. Effective Communication: The Bridge Between People and Ideas

   It is often said that communication is the lifeblood of leadership. I used to think this just meant being good at giving presentations or sending clear emails. But the real art of communication is understanding how to convey complex technical concepts to non-technical stakeholders and vice versa. As a leader, you need to translate between different "languages"—the language of your developers, your managers, and your clients.

There was a moment in my career when this lesson hit home. We were facing a delay in product launch due to unforeseen technical challenges. The technical team was deep into jargon, while the production, sales, and service teams panicked about missed targets. My job was not just to relay facts but to bridge the understanding gap. I had to explain the delay in a way that made sense to the sales team without making the engineers feel like they had failed.

Challenge yourself: Next time you communicate, consider who you are talking to. Are you making your point in a way that they will understand and value?

5. Resilience and Persistence: The Backbone of Leadership

The path to leadership is not a straight line, and it certainly is not without setbacks. In IT, we deal with constant pressure—tight deadlines, evolving technologies, and complex problems. The real test of a leader is not how they handle success but how they navigate failure.

In one of my most challenging projects, we faced repeated setbacks. Deadlines were missed, features were not working as expected, and the team was demoralized. It would have been easy to give in to frustration, but I knew that as the leader, I had to remain resilient. I encouraged my team to see every obstacle as a learning opportunity. We pushed forward, and though the final product was not exactly what we envisioned, it ended up being more innovative and effective than we could have imagined.

Reflect on this: How do you handle failure? Do you encourage your team to persist and learn from setbacks, or do you get discouraged easily?

Transitioning from Individual Contributor to Leader

One of the hardest transitions for any mid-career IT professional is moving from an individual contributor to leadership. I have been there, and it is a difficult shift. Suddenly, it is not just about the code you write or the bugs you fix – it is about the team you lead and the direction you provide.

I remember struggling with delegation. I wanted to keep my hands in technical work because that is where I was comfortable. But as I grew into my leadership role, I learned that empowering others was more valuable than doing everything myself. The more I trusted my team, the more they delivered.

Ask yourself: Am I still trying to do everything myself? How can I better empower my team?

Conclusion: Building Leadership in IT

Becoming a successful leader in IT requires more than just mastering technology. It demands emotional intelligence, adaptability, visionary thinking, effective communication, and resilience. These are not just traits you develop overnight—they are skills you build over time through experience and self-reflection.

Leadership is not about knowing all the answers. It is about guiding your team through the uncertainty and challenges that arise in the ever-changing world of IT. It is about creating an environment where your team feels valued, motivated, and empowered to innovate and execute.

And remember, as you grow into leadership, the journey does not stop. In fact, it is just beginning. The next chapter in this book will delve deeper into one of the most critical aspects of long-term success: **Continuous Learning and Staying Relevant.** In an industry that is evolving every second, the best leaders are those who never stop learning. So, how will you ensure that both you and your team continue to grow?

Chapter 6

Continuous Learning and Staying Relevant

The importance of staying updated in a rapidly evolving tech landscape.

Identifying the right learning paths, skills, and certifications.

Balancing continuous learning with day-to-day responsibilities.

The Importance of Staying Updated in a Rapidly Evolving Tech Landscape

The tech industry is a whirlwind, constantly morphing with each passing day. New technologies like artificial intelligence, cloud computing, and blockchain emerge breathtakingly, leaving many mid-career professionals feeling overwhelmed. We often find ourselves juggling the demands of our daily responsibilities while trying to keep our skills relevant. This struggle can be daunting, but it is crucial for our growth and success.

I remember the day I stood before my peers after earning my Executive MBA—a milestone I pursued nearly two decades into my career. The faces of my classmates reflected both exhaustion and exhilaration. Some had just transitioned from technical roles to management, while others were eyeing leadership positions. It struck me then that we were all navigating similar waters. We had grown comfortable, but comfort can be a trap. Just as a tree must be nourished to flourish, we too must embrace continuous learning to thrive in this fast-paced environment.

1. The Tech Landscape: A Constant State of Change

The rapid evolution of technology is both exciting and intimidating. Remember when cloud computing was just a buzzword? Ten years ago, I watched as many organizations clung to outdated, on-premises infrastructures. Fast forward to today, and cloud solutions are fundamental. Professionals who embraced the change and invested in learning cloud technologies like Amazon Web Services (AWS) and Azure found themselves not only surviving but thriving. Those who resisted, however, often found their skills becoming obsolete.

The reality is the tech landscape requires us to be proficient in various disciplines. Understanding data analytics and cloud infrastructure has become as essential as coding. Continuous learning is not merely about keeping up with trends but developing a diverse skill set that includes leadership and strategic thinking.

2. Continuous Learning: A Game-Changer for Mid-Career Professionals

It is easy to become complacent. After years of dedication, we might focus solely on our current roles, ignoring the need for growth. But this mindset can hinder our career advancement.

For example, I once met a talented engineer, Vijaya, who had over a decade of experience in software development. Despite her skills, she struggled to move into management roles. She realized that her technical prowess alone was not enough. Vijaya transformed her career by embracing continuous learning, attending workshops, and networking. She developed the strategic insight needed to lead teams, ultimately stepping into a management position. Her journey taught me that learning is not just about knowledge; it is a catalyst for change.

> "The more that you read, the more things
> you will know. The more that you learn,
> the more places you'll go."
> — Dr. Seuss

3. Nurturing Yourself for the Next Big Role

Staying relevant means preparing for the challenges ahead. As mid-career professionals, we should proactively shape our careers. Continuous learning nurtures us, preparing us for bigger challenges and more fulfilling roles.

Even dedicating just 20 minutes a day to learning—be it reading industry articles or taking short online courses—can yield significant benefits. Consider this: What if you engaged with a tech podcast or enrolled in a new course instead of scrolling through social media? This small shift in habit could elevate your career.

4. Making Learning a Priority

Learning often falls by the wayside in our busy lives. However, in the tech field, it must be a priority. Dedicating time to learning through structured courses or informal discussions keeps us competitive and agile.

Let me share my experience attending an industry conference last year. I went in with a vague idea of what I wanted to learn but left with many insights and new connections. Engaging in conversations allowed me to absorb knowledge and contribute my own perspectives. Sometimes, these informal exchanges spark the biggest ideas and opportunities.

5. Staying Connected with the Industry

Staying updated involves more than just individual learning; it requires staying connected with the industry. Attend conferences, seminars, and networking events to gain insights into emerging trends.

I often recall my first networking event, where I felt like an outsider. However, as I engaged with others and shared my experiences, I began to see the value of those connections. The relationships I formed opened doors I never imagined, proving that staying connected to the pulse of the industry can lead to unexpected opportunities.

6. Embrace a Lifelong Learning Mindset

The most vital takeaway is to embrace a lifelong learning mindset. Change is constant in the tech industry, and those who view learning as a journey will always have an advantage. Do not wait until your skills feel outdated; be proactive. Cultivate curiosity and seek out new information.

Conclusion of this topic: Stay Relevant, Stay Ahead

As mid-career professionals, our value extends beyond what we know. Our ability to stay updated and continuously learn prepares us for growth and makes us invaluable to our organizations. Continuous learning is not just a choice; it is essential.

As we transition into identifying the right learning paths, skills, and certifications, let's commit to making learning a daily habit. The investment you make in yourself today will pay dividends throughout your career. Remember, the learning journey is ongoing; embrace it with open arms.

Identifying the Right Learning Paths, Skills, and Certifications

In the ever-evolving technology landscape, mid-career professionals often find themselves at a crossroads: How can I stay relevant and competitive? The decisions we make regarding skill acquisition and certifications significantly shape our career trajectories. Choosing the right learning path is not a mere checklist; it is a journey of strategic introspection, market awareness, and a clear vision for the future.

Reflecting on my two-decade journey, I recall a pivotal moment when I realized the power of continuous learning. Early in my career, I earned a Master's in Embedded Systems, but it was not until I pursued an Executive MBA a decade later that I truly grasped how structured learning could fuel my ambition. This was not just about collecting degrees but about adapting and thriving in a rapidly changing world.

1. Align Learning with Career Goals

Imagine standing at a fork in the road, where each path represents a potential future. Which direction do you choose? Aligning your learning with your career goals is essential. Mid-career professionals may have achieved milestones, but where do you want to go next?

Are you aiming for a leadership role, a technical specialization, or perhaps a lateral move into a different industry? Ask yourself these questions. For example, when I aspired to transition into strategic decision-making, pursuing an Executive MBA was a game-changer. This choice was not random but a deliberate step toward my long-term aspirations.

Take a moment to reflect:

What are your long-term career aspirations?

What industry trends are emerging that resonate with your goals?

Who can you reach out to for guidance?

2. Choose Skills That Add Value

After aligning your learning with your goals, it is time to select the skills that will set you apart. Not all skills are created equal; the value of a skill can vary significantly depending on your industry and role.

Consider a technology firm undergoing digital transformation. Skills like cloud computing, AI, and cybersecurity are not just buzzwords but vital for survival. If you are in leadership, focus on emotional intelligence and strategic decision-making.

In my own experience, staying attuned to organizational goals has helped me prioritize skills that matter. When I noticed a growing emphasis on business strategy in technology roles, I prioritized relevant courses and certifications.

Reflect on your context:

Which skills would elevate your current role?

How can you enhance your organization's performance through your learning?

3. Leverage Certifications for Credibility

Certifications can be a powerful asset, signaling to employers that you have validated skills. However, pursue certifications strategically; chasing after many without focus can dilute your efforts.

Consider certifications from recognized bodies like PMI, AWS, or Google. When I transitioned from technical roles to leadership, obtaining my PMP, and Scrum Master Certification boosted my credibility and prepared me to lead agile teams effectively. This journey was not just about a certification but about equipping myself to navigate leadership challenges in a fast-paced environment.

Ask yourself:

Which certifications align with your career trajectory?

Are there industry-preferred certifications you should prioritize?

4. Utilize Learning Platforms and Communities

In today's digital age, online learning platforms offer unprecedented access to high-quality education. Platforms like Coursera, edX, and LinkedIn Learning provide flexibility and a wide array of courses.

Engaging in professional networks and attending meetups can also be invaluable. They are not just about learning; they are about building connections. When I attended a tech summit and shared insights with industry leaders, it opened doors I did not know existed.

Consider your next steps:

What online platforms can you explore for skill development?

Are there local or virtual meetups you can attend to network and learn?

5. Embrace Continuous Learning

Learning does not end with a certification. In the tech landscape, evolution is constant. Make learning a habit—dedicate time weekly to staying updated. Whether it is reading industry reports or attending webinars, this commitment will keep your skills sharp and prepare you for future challenges.

As we wrap up, I encourage you to apply these insights to your unique journey. The path of learning is one of exploration, adaptation, and growth.

In my experience, the continuous learning journey is filled with unexpected turns, but each turn leads to new opportunities. As we dive into the next section, we'll explore **"Balancing Continuous Learning with Day-to-Day Responsibilities."** How can you integrate learning into your busy life without feeling overwhelmed? Let's discover practical strategies to achieve that balance together.

Balancing Continuous Learning with Day-to-Day Responsibilities

Balancing Continuous Learning with Life's Demands

As mid-career professionals, we find ourselves at a crossroads—juggling the demands of managing projects, leading teams, and fulfilling stakeholder expectations while keeping pace in an ever-evolving industry. Amid this whirlwind, continuous learning often feels like an unattainable goal, yet it is not just a luxury; it is essential for both our careers and personal fulfillment.

Having spent over two decades in the tech industry, I can attest to the power of learning as a transformative force. During my journey, I earned two master's degrees while working full-time, including a Master of Science in Embedded Systems and an Executive MBA. The challenge was not merely recognizing the importance of learning; it was about weaving it into the fabric of my daily life without sacrificing my responsibilities or personal time.

Prioritize Learning: Make It Non-Negotiable

First and foremost, treat learning as a non-negotiable task. Just as we carve out time for important meetings or project deadlines, we need to schedule our learning sessions. This approach not only elevates the importance of learning but also helps establish a routine.

While pursuing my Executive MBA, I learned to block specific times in my calendar for studying—sacred slots that

I protected fiercely. In one instance, a crucial work project threatened to encroach on my study time. Instead of yielding, I communicated with my team about my commitment to learning, ensuring they understood its significance. This discipline helped me maintain a balance that was rewarding both professionally and personally.

Interactive Tip: Consider your calendar. Where can you carve out even 20-30 minutes daily for focused learning? It can be as simple as integrating a podcast during your commute or designating a quiet time before bed for reading.

Set Realistic Goals: Small Steps Lead to Big Wins

Learning can feel overwhelming, especially when we set lofty goals. Instead of mastering an entire skill set at once, break your goals into manageable pieces. I remember tackling artificial intelligence and machine learning while leading a team. Rather than trying to digest everything at once, I focused on one subtopic at a time. Each week, I would dive deeper, celebrating each small victory. This strategy not only minimized burnout but also made the process enjoyable.

Interactive Challenge: Set a specific learning goal for the week, such as completing one module of an online course. Track your progress and reward yourself with a small treat upon completion. This reinforces a positive learning loop.

Leverage On-the-Job Learning Opportunities

Integrating learning into your daily work can be an effective strategy. Often, we overlook the rich opportunities available in our current roles. During a project, I volunteered to lead an initiative involving unfamiliar technology. Embracing this challenge allowed me to grow technically and enhanced my leadership skills. It taught me that each responsibility could become a learning experience.

Interactive Suggestion: What stretch assignments can you pursue at work? Consider volunteering for a project that pushes your boundaries, whether through new technologies or methodologies. Embrace the chance to learn while contributing.

Embrace a Growth Mindset

Adopting a growth mindset is crucial. Viewing learning as a journey fosters resilience and encourages you to view setbacks as opportunities for growth. I have had moments when life's demands limited my learning time, but rather than feeling discouraged, I focused on small, consistent efforts. Each time I learned something new, I reminded myself that progress—no matter how incremental—is still progress.

> "Success is the sum of small efforts,
> repeated day in and day out."
> — Robert Collier

Interactive Reflection: Reflect on a recent challenge you faced in your learning journey. What did you learn from it?

Write down three lessons that emerged from that experience and consider how you can apply them moving forward.

Delegate and Automate: Free Up Your Time

Feeling overwhelmed? It is time to delegate and automate. By shifting non-essential tasks off your plate, you free up valuable time to focus on learning. In my leadership roles, I learned to trust my team with day-to-day tasks, allowing me to concentrate on strategic initiatives and continuous learning. **Automation tools became my allies in managing routine tasks, creating precious time for what truly** matters.

Remembered The Eisenhower Matrix is also known as the time management matrix?

The Eisenhower Box, and the urgent-important matrix. This tool helps you divide your tasks into four categories: the tasks you'll do first, the tasks you'll schedule for later, the tasks you'll delegate, and the tasks you'll delete.

Interactive Exercise: Identify one task this week that you can delegate to someone else or automate using a tool. Monitor how this shift impacts your available time for learning.

Conclusion: Continuous Learning is a Marathon, Not a Sprint

Balancing continuous learning with daily responsibilities demands strategy and discipline. Remember, learning is a marathon, not a sprint. As mid-career professionals, we hold the reins to shape our careers through this investment in growth.

By prioritizing learning, setting realistic goals, leveraging on-the-job opportunities, embracing a growth mindset, and strategically freeing up time, we can navigate our responsibilities while expanding our knowledge and skills.

In the next chapter, we'll explore **Overcoming Challenges and Pushing Boundaries**, delving into how to confront obstacles head-on and emerge stronger. Every challenge presents a chance for growth—let's embrace them together.

Part 4

Overcoming Challenges and Pushing Boundaries

Chapter 7

Self-Development and Building the Right Habits

The habits of successful mid-career IT professionals.

Developing a growth-oriented mindset.

Emotional Intelligence: The Bedrock of Self-Development and Leadership

How to manage time, energy, and focus effectively.

- **"Have you ever wondered what sets apart mid-career professionals who continue to excel from those who plateau? Could it be that their habits, rather than just their skills, hold the key to sustained success?"**

- **"What daily habits are you cultivating to ensure you're not just keeping up in your IT career but consistently staying ahead of the curve?**

The habits of successful mid-career IT professionals.

Reflecting on my journey over the past few years, one thing stands out: cultivating new habits completely transformed my productivity, energy, and outlook. Like many mid-career professionals, I once thought I was too busy to develop new habits. But here is the truth: the time is there—you just need to find it. A hard look at where your time goes each day will reveal hidden pockets you can repurpose.

Let me share one of the first habits I embraced—reading regularly. A few years ago, I could barely get through a book. I would read a few pages and lose momentum. It felt daunting. But, like training for a marathon, I started small, reading for just 10 minutes a day. Over time, my endurance grew, and now, reading has become a part of my daily routine. The knowledge I have gained from those books has played a vital role in my personal and career growth.

Running was another hurdle I overcame. I had always been a sprinter, grabbed many prizes in running races during school and college time and believed I could not run long distances. It was a mental block more than a physical one. But by pushing my boundaries bit by bit, I started running farther. Eventually, I ran a half marathon—something I never imagined myself doing. This taught me a key lesson: we impose limitations on ourselves that can be shattered with discipline and persistence.

The same goes for writing. I never saw myself as a writer. The idea of creating content that resonates with others felt intimidating. But I pushed through, starting with small posts and gradually writing longer articles. Today, writing is not only a tool for communication but a way to clarify my thoughts and share my experiences with others in the industry.

What do these examples have in common? They all stem from embracing habits that took me out of my comfort zone. And that is where the real growth happens. As mid-career professionals, we often get stuck in routines, thinking that if we are good at something, we should just keep doing it. But that is not how we evolve. We need habits that challenge us, push us forward, and open new possibilities.

1. Lifelong Learning

The first habit is continuous learning. In our fast-paced industry, staying still is equivalent to falling behind. Whether through online courses, certifications, or industry events, carving out time to learn is essential. It does not have to be hours—just 20 minutes a day can make a world of difference. In my case, I pursued a Master's in Embedded Systems after seven years in the field. Later, I went for an Executive MBA. Lifelong learning has not just kept me relevant; it has prepared me for the next step in my career.

Action Point: Think about one skill or topic you have always wanted to learn. Could you carve out 20 minutes a day to start building that knowledge?

2. Setting Clear, Attainable Goals

Successful professionals do not just go with the flow – they chart their course. I used to believe that doing my job well was enough, but everything changed when I started setting specific career goals. With clear targets, I could move from short-term tasks to a long-term strategy for my career. Every goal achieved is a step closer to a larger vision.

Action Point: What is your next career milestone? Write it down, break it into smaller tasks, and work on it bit by bit.

3. Embracing New Challenges

Comfort is the enemy of growth. If everything feels easy, it is time to seek new challenges. Early in my career, I hesitated to take on big initiatives, thinking I might fail. But I quickly learned that every challenge faced builds new skills, visibility, and opportunities. Whether it is leading a project or solving a complex problem, each one stretches your capabilities.

Action Point: Ask yourself, "What's one challenge I can take on that will push me out of my comfort zone?" Then act on it.

4. Reflection and Improvement

The final habit is regular self-reflection. Successful professionals are constantly assessing their progress and asking themselves how they can improve. Personally, I take time each week to reflect on what went well and what I could do better. This habit of introspection has allowed me to continuously fine-tune my approach, both personally and professionally.

Action Point: At the end of your week, reflect on what you achieved and what could be better. Make a small adjustment for the next week.

Daily habits are the foundation of long-term success, and I have experienced their transformative power firsthand. A few years ago, I felt overwhelmed, constantly chasing deadlines without a clear focus. That is when I began incorporating small, consistent habits like meditation, reading for 20 minutes a day, and exercising. These daily rituals grounded me, helping me stay connected with both my mind and body.

Take meditation, for example. It is more than just a pause—it is a reset. It helps me clear mental clutter and reconnect with my purpose. Leaders like Jeff Weiner, former CEO of LinkedIn, swear by it. Meditation has been a game-changer for him, improving focus and decision-making. Personally, it has allowed me to approach challenges with a clearer, calmer mind.

Equally important is spending quality time with family. Every day, I make it a point to disconnect from work and truly engage with loved ones for at least an hour. This time not only recharges me but also brings a sense of balance that enhances my productivity.

Action Point: What one daily habit can you add today—whether it is 10 minutes of meditation, reading, or time with family—that will bring clarity and boost your productivity?

Building these habits—learning, goal setting, embracing challenges, and reflecting—has helped me redefine my career path. As you think about your own, ask yourself: What habits are holding you back? And, more importantly, what new habits can you build to unlock your potential?

Next, let's explore how developing a **growth-oriented mindset** can further propel your career and personal growth.

Developing a growth-oriented mindset:

As I reflect on my own professional journey, I can pinpoint the moment my career truly began to accelerate; it was when I adopted a growth-oriented mindset. Reading books such as *Attitude is Everything* by Jeff Keller and *Mindset: The New Psychology of Success* by Carol Dweck fundamentally reshaped my thought process. These books helped me shift from a fixed mindset—where I believed my abilities were static and predetermined—to a growth mindset, which empowered me to think and act on a much larger scale.

It is easy to fall into the trap of believing that we are limited by our innate abilities or by the environment we are in. Many mid-career professionals, after years of executing the same tasks, begin to feel that their career trajectory has plateaued. But here is the reality: your mindset can either be your greatest asset or your biggest roadblock. As Dweck explains in her book, individuals with a fixed mindset believe that their talents and intelligence are set in stone, which often leads them to avoid challenges and shy away from opportunities for growth. On the other hand, those with a growth mindset view challenges as opportunities to improve and develop new skills, unlocking doors to professional and personal advancement.

When I embraced the growth mindset, it shifted my perspective dramatically. Suddenly, every challenge was a stepping stone, every failure a lesson. Instead of looking at limitations, I started to focus on possibilities. This shift was not just theoretical—it led me to take actions I had not previously considered. I started thinking in terms of 10x, asking myself, "How can I multiply my efforts, my skills, and my contributions?" This mindset allowed me to break through barriers that had held me back, both in my career and personal development.

The good news is that anyone can develop a growth mindset. It is not a trait you are born with; it is something you cultivate through consistent effort and practice. Below are five practical steps to help mid-career professionals adopt a growth-oriented mindset and accelerate their personal and professional growth.

1. Embrace Challenges

One of the most defining traits of a growth-oriented mindset is the willingness to embrace challenges. When you view challenges as opportunities to learn and grow, you no longer shy away from them. Instead, you actively seek them out. This mindset shift requires you to move beyond your comfort zone and put yourself in situations where you will be stretched and tested.

Take the example of Satya Nadella, CEO of Microsoft. Nadella stepped into leadership at a time when Microsoft was struggling to regain its footing in an ever-evolving tech landscape. Instead of avoiding the significant challenges ahead, he embraced them with a deep understanding of the company's needs and the people within it. He didn't just focus on strategy but took time to listen, empathize, and understand the emotional toll that uncertainty was taking on his team. Nadella's growth-oriented mindset led him to pivot Microsoft's focus toward cloud computing and AI, even though the company was initially behind its competitors. His ability to inspire with empathy, resilience, and vision helped not only steer Microsoft back to prominence but also create an environment where employees felt valued and motivated to contribute to the company's redefining journey. Nadella's leadership wasn't just about innovation—it was about leading with heart, ensuring that people were at the core of every change.

For mid-career professionals, this means not waiting for challenges to come to you but actively seeking out complex projects and problems to solve. Whether it is learning a new technology, taking on a new leadership role, or venturing into uncharted territory, embracing challenges is a key driver of growth.

"Success is not final, failure is not fatal:
It is the courage to continue that counts."
— Winston Churchill

2. Learn from Feedback

A growth-oriented mindset thrives on feedback. In a fixed mindset, feedback is often viewed as a personal attack, while in a growth mindset, feedback is seen as an opportunity to improve. By seeking and accepting constructive criticism, you can adjust your approach and continuously grow.

Sheryl Sandberg, COO of Meta, has always been a strong advocate for embracing feedback. In her book *Lean In*, she emphasizes the importance of asking for feedback even when it is hard to hear. In one instance, she talks about how Mark Zuckerberg told her she was "too critical" in her feedback with others. Instead of taking this personally, Sandberg internalized the feedback and adjusted her approach, allowing her to become a more effective leader.

For mid-career professionals, this means actively seeking feedback from mentors, peers, and supervisors. This feedback loop will help you identify blind spots and areas for improvement, allowing you to become a more effective and dynamic professional.

3. Cultivate Persistence

Another key aspect of the growth mindset is persistence. In *Mindset*, Carol Dweck shares the story of Thomas Edison, who is often quoted as saying, *"I have not failed. I've just found 10,000 ways that won't work."* Edison's persistence in the face of repeated failure exemplifies the growth mindset. Each setback was considered valuable information rather than a reason to give up.

Persistence is essential for mid-career professionals. Whether you are working on a long-term project, transitioning into a new role, or trying to develop new skills, the road to success is often filled with obstacles. The key is to persist through these challenges, viewing each failure as an opportunity to learn and grow.

In my own experience, I faced multiple challenges in building habits that supported my growth. Whether it was struggling to read more efficiently or breaking through the mental barrier of running long distances, persistence helped me overcome my self-imposed limitations. The growth mindset enabled me to stay the course, knowing that each small step forward brought me closer to my goals.

4. Focus on Continuous Learning

Successful mid-career professionals understand that learning is not a one-time event but a lifelong journey. In today's fast-paced tech industry, staying relevant requires a commitment to continuous learning. This mindset ensures that you are always improving, expanding your knowledge base, and staying ahead of the curve.

Indra Nooyi, the former CEO of PepsiCo, is a prime example of a leader who prioritizes continuous learning. Despite her demanding career, Nooyi was known for constantly reading and learning about new industries and ideas, ensuring that she could adapt and innovate within her role.

For mid-career professionals, this could mean pursuing certifications, enrolling in advanced courses, or simply reading regularly to stay updated with industry trends. By making learning a priority, you not only improve your skills but also position yourself for future opportunities.

5. Surround Yourself with Growth-Minded People

One of the most powerful ways to cultivate a growth mindset is by surrounding yourself with people who share that mentality. When you are in an environment where growth, innovation, and personal development are encouraged, it becomes easier to adopt and maintain a growth mindset yourself.

Steve Jobs was known for surrounding himself with people who challenged him and pushed him to think differently. He sought out team members and mentors who would not simply agree with him but would push him to explore new ideas and take calculated risks. This environment of growth and innovation was a significant factor in Apple's success.

As a mid-career professional, this might mean finding mentors, joining industry groups, or building a network of like-minded peers. These connections will provide you with new perspectives, insights, and encouragement to continue growing.

Adopting a Growth-Oriented Mindset

Developing a growth-oriented mindset is one of the most valuable things you can do as a mid-career professional. It allows you to break through limitations, continuously improve, and embrace new challenges. Whether through cultivating persistence, seeking feedback, or surrounding yourself with growth-minded individuals, this mindset will push you beyond your comfort zone and open doors to new opportunities.

The five-step process outlined here—embracing challenges, learning from feedback, cultivating persistence, focusing on continuous learning, and surrounding yourself with growth-minded people—will not only help you achieve your current goals but will also prepare you for the next phase of your career. By adopting these practices, you will be equipped to take on bigger challenges, make more significant contributions, and experience exponential growth in your personal and professional life.

Emotional Intelligence: The Bedrock of Self-Development and Leadership

Emotional Intelligence (EQ) is a core element of effective leadership and personal growth. In the fast-paced, often high-stress tech industry, EQ has become a must-have skill. But what makes it so essential for mid-career professionals aiming for leadership? EQ is the ability to understand, manage, and harness emotions—both one's own and those of others—to guide thinking, behavior, and relationships in a constructive direction. For professionals navigating their way through complex projects, high-stakes decisions, and team dynamics, a high EQ often marks the difference between merely managing tasks and inspiring others.

> "Your emotions are the slaves to your thoughts,
> and you are the slave to your emotions."
> –Elizabeth Gilbert

The Importance of Emotional Intelligence in the Tech Industry

As careers progress, technical skills become less of a differentiator and leadership and relational skills take precedence. Emotional intelligence impacts several dimensions that are key to success at this stage:

Effective Decision-Making: Leaders with high EQ approach decision-making not only with data but also with a keen understanding of the human factors at play, leading to better-rounded, lasting solutions. For example, a project manager who needs to reorganize team roles due to budget constraints will make wiser, more compassionate decisions if they consider the team's morale and career goals.

Team Collaboration: Emotional intelligence enhances collaboration by improving communication, empathy, and trust. When leaders can read emotions accurately and respond thoughtfully, they create environments where people feel understood and motivated. In an industry where collaborative innovation is key, this skill cannot be overlooked.

Resilience in High-Pressure Situations: Leaders in IT often face tight deadlines and high expectations. High EQ equips them to manage stress effectively, keep their focus sharp, and remain resilient through setbacks, all of which inspire their teams to maintain productivity and morale.

Building High EQ: A Necessary Skill for Great Leaders

Developing high EQ is not an overnight journey, but it is an achievable one. Here is a step-by-step framework for strengthening EQ as part of personal and professional development:

1. **Self-Awareness: The Starting Point**

   Self-awareness is foundational to emotional intelligence. It involves recognizing one's emotions, triggers, strengths, and areas of improvement. This awareness helps professionals avoid reactive decisions and allows for a thoughtful, composed approach.

   Example: Consider a scenario where a product lead is blindsided by an urgent client request just before a deadline. Rather than reacting with frustration, a self-aware leader recognizes their initial emotions and takes a moment to regroup before addressing the situation with composure. This measured response often leads to more rational, strategic choices.

How to Develop Self-Awareness:

Practice Reflection: Set aside a few minutes each day to reflect on your emotions, decisions, and reactions. Document any patterns or recurring triggers.

Seek Feedback: Regular feedback from peers, mentors, or team members can provide insight into blind spots and areas for improvement.

Mindfulness Exercises: Techniques like mindfulness meditation can enhance your ability to recognize emotions as they arise, improving your response control.

2. **Self-Regulation: Controlling Emotional Reactions**

Self-regulation is the ability to manage your emotional responses, especially during stressful situations. In the tech world, where the unexpected is common, self-regulation helps prevent knee-jerk reactions and instead fosters a controlled, thoughtful response.

Example: Imagine a team leader whose project deadline has been pushed forward unexpectedly. Instead of venting or panicking, a leader with self-regulation stays calm, focuses on potential solutions, and calmly reassigns resources or responsibilities to meet the new deadline.

How to Build Self-Regulation:

Pause and Assess: In high-stress situations, take a brief pause to collect your thoughts before responding.

Develop Positive Outlets: Physical exercise, journaling, or talking with a mentor can help manage stress, making it easier to self-regulate in difficult moments.

Set Clear Personal Values: Define your principles and standards. These values can serve as a guide when making challenging decisions, making it easier to stay composed.

3. **Empathy: Understanding Others' Perspectives.**

   Empathy is the capacity to see things from another person's viewpoint. This skill is invaluable in leading a diverse team, understanding stakeholder needs, and making thoughtful decisions that resonate well with others.

   Example: A development lead notices that a team member has become withdrawn and unproductive. Rather than assuming laziness, an empathetic leader takes time to check in, discovering that the team member is struggling with personal challenges. By offering understanding and support, the leader not only helps the individual regain their focus but also builds a more trusting team environment.

   How to Cultivate Empathy:

   Listen Actively: In conversations, focus fully on what the other person is saying. Avoid interrupting or planning your response while they are speaking.

Practice Perspective-Taking: Try to put yourself in the other person's shoes, considering their background, responsibilities, and current pressures.

Encourage Open Communication: Create a work culture where team members feel safe sharing challenges and ideas without fear of judgment or retaliation.

4. **Social Skills: Building Meaningful Connections**

Effective leaders use their social skills to build strong professional relationships, manage conflict, and foster a collaborative work culture. In industries where team success often hinges on solid interpersonal dynamics, these skills are critical.

Example: A product manager needs input from various departments to complete a project. Leaders with strong social skills can engage people across different functions, encourage input, and build a sense of ownership among team members, enhancing collaboration and output quality.

Steps to Enhance Social Skills:

Develop Conflict Resolution Skills: Learn to address conflicts early and constructively, finding solutions that satisfy all parties.

Show Appreciation: Recognize team members' achievements and efforts, fostering goodwill and encouraging a positive, productive work environment.

Engage Authentically: Take time to build genuine connections with colleagues, which improves trust and makes teamwork more effective.

5. Motivation: The Drive to Succeed

Motivated leaders inspire their teams to go the extra mile. They are focused on personal goals, organizational vision, and team success, creating a culture of purpose and achievement.

Example: A senior developer consistently works to improve team productivity by streamlining code review processes. Their passion for optimizing team performance motivates colleagues to adopt best practices and contributes to a collaborative environment focused on continuous improvement.

How to Boost Motivation:

Set Personal and Professional Goals: Regularly establish challenging yet attainable goals that push you to grow.

Celebrate Milestones: Recognize achievements, both personal and team-related, to maintain morale and momentum.

Find Purpose: Connect your work to a larger mission. Understanding how your role impacts the broader goals of the organization can enhance your drive to succeed.

Emotional Intelligence as a Competitive Advantage.

Incorporating high EQ into your professional toolkit is not just a way to improve interactions; it is a competitive advantage in today's complex workplace. Leaders with high emotional intelligence are more adaptable, resilient, and trusted by their teams. They foster environments where people feel valued and heard, leading to higher productivity, innovation, and loyalty. By following this framework and intentionally developing your EQ skills, you will find that personal and professional success becomes not only achievable but sustainable.

Embracing EQ as part of self-development and building the right habits can set mid-career professionals on a path towards transformative leadership, with benefits that ripple through teams, projects, and entire organizations.

How to Manage Time, Energy, and Focus Effectively – The 4-Letter Framework

Mid-career professionals often find themselves at a pivotal point where managing time, energy, and focus becomes critical to not only maintaining but also accelerating their career growth. In a high-paced, tech-driven environment, it can feel overwhelming to balance multiple projects, continuous learning, leadership responsibilities, and personal life. To thrive at this stage, you need a practical and personalized approach to managing these resources. Through my own journey, I have realized that it is not just about putting in more hours but about working smarter by maximizing your time, energy, and focus.

Here, simple 4-letter framework to help mid-career professionals optimize their productivity: **PLAN (Prioritize, Limt distractions, Allocate Energy wisely, Nurture Consistency).** This simple, actionable method will ensure you manage your most valuable resources effectively while aligning them with your career goals.

P: Prioritize

The first step to managing your time and energy is knowing what to prioritize. As a mid-career professional, you are likely juggling numerous responsibilities, but not all tasks carry the same weight. Learn to differentiate between urgent and important tasks. The Eisenhower Matrix is an effective tool that helps you categorize your tasks into four quadrants: urgent and important, important but not urgent, urgent but not important, and neither urgent nor important. Your goal should be to focus on what is important but not necessarily urgent.

For example, during one of my projects, I found myself constantly bombarded with emails and meetings. I felt like I was running on a treadmill without getting anywhere. That is when I applied this principle to break down my tasks and prioritize what truly moved the needle. As soon as I focused on high-impact activities—like strategic planning and team development—my productivity soared.

Tip: Start your day by identifying the top three priorities that align with your larger career goals. Ask yourself, "What are the three things I can do today that will push me closer to where I want to be in the next year?"

L: Limit Distractions

Distractions are the archenemy of focus. Especially in the mid-career phase, where your responsibilities often span across multiple areas, it is easy to get distracted by emails, meetings, and even social media. The key to managing your focus is limiting distractions through proactive measures.

One of the techniques I found incredibly useful is time-blocking. By dedicating specific blocks of time to deep work, you can minimize distractions and concentrate on the task at hand. For instance, when I was writing reports or working on critical projects, I would block out 2-3 hours of focused time in my calendar and turn off all notifications. This allowed me to dive into complex tasks without interruption.

Example: Sheryl Sandberg, COO of Meta, is a firm believer in managing focus by limiting distractions. She once shared in an interview that she used to make time for emails early in the morning and after work hours, while the bulk of her day was spent in focused, strategic thinking sessions.

Tip: Try turning off notifications for an hour each day and observe the difference in your productivity. You will be amazed at how much deep work you can accomplish without distractions.

A: Allocate Energy Wisely

Time management alone is not enough—managing your energy is equally important. Have you ever noticed how some tasks feel effortless in the morning while others drain you in the afternoon? That is because your energy levels fluctuate throughout the day. The secret to staying productive is aligning your energy with the right tasks.

For instance, I discovered that my peak productivity times were early morning and late afternoon. During these windows, I scheduled my most mentally demanding tasks, such as strategic planning or problem-solving. On the other hand, I reserved administrative tasks, like emails or status updates, for energy dips during the midday slump.

Tip: Identify your peak energy times and schedule high-priority, deep-focus tasks during those hours. Reserve less critical activities for when your energy naturally wanes.

N: Nurture Consistency

The final element of the PLAN framework is nurturing consistency. Consistency compounds over time. Whether it is building new skills, managing teams, or pursuing long-term projects, consistent effort is what drives exponential growth. The key to consistency lies in building sustainable habits that keep you moving forward, even when motivation wanes.

When I started incorporating the habit of reading daily into my routine, I found it challenging to stick to it at first. But by committing to just 15-20 minutes of reading each day, I eventually built it into a consistent practice. Over time, this habit allowed me to stay updated on industry trends, improve my strategic thinking, and even shift my mindset towards continuous learning.

Example: Bill Gates is known for his habit of "Think Weeks," where he dedicates an entire week twice a year to deep reading and thinking. He attributes much of his long-term success to this consistent practice, which keeps him informed and ready to tackle complex challenges.

Tip: Start by building one small habit and stick to it. Whether it is learning a new skill, reading, or writing, consistency will eventually lead to mastery.

Conclusion

In the fast-evolving world of tech, mastering time, energy, and focus is essential for mid-career professionals aiming for growth. By applying the **PLAN** framework—Prioritizing tasks, Limiting distractions, Allocating energy wisely, and Nurturing consistency—you will be able to make tangible progress toward your goals without burning out.

Remember, it is not just about working harder; it is about working smarter. When you learn to manage your time, energy, and focus effectively, you open the door to exponential growth and long-term career success.

Chapter 8

Getting Out of Your Comfort Zone

How staying too comfortable can hinder career growth.

Examples of professionals who took risks to accelerate their careers.

Practical steps to push beyond your comfort zone for exponential growth.

- **"Have you ever wondered why your career feels stagnant despite years of hard work? Could it be that you're stuck in the comfort zone, afraid to take on the challenges that lead to growth?"**

- **"What if the only thing holding you back from your next big career breakthrough is your unwillingness to step outside the boundaries of what feels safe and familiar?"**

Bang on, you absolutely got your answer... these are the right symptoms you sensed.

Let me get started. When you are too comfortable at work, doing your job with ease, and being very productive, it means that you have already mastered it. This does not mean that you will always grow or get the next promotion, and the truth is it will not take you far. Have you started working on getting your next job while being in your current role? Staying too at ease at work may not help your growth; it will hinder it. Sometimes, you may be overdoing it and not learning much. If you are absolutely sure that you can finish any kind of work in your current job, it means you are not facing many challenges in your current role.

Breaking Free from Career Stagnation by Embracing New Challenges

You have probably asked yourself:

"Why does my career feel stagnant despite years of hard work?"

"I'm doing everything right, so why do I feel stuck?"

Chances are, if you are in a mid-career phase and feeling like progress has come to a halt, it is because you have become comfortable—maybe too comfortable. While comfort can be a good thing, giving us a sense of security, it is also a dangerous place when it comes to long-term growth and career advancement. Comfort does not drive transformation; discomfort does.

The Hidden Trap of Mastery

At this stage in your career, you have likely mastered your role. You handle daily tasks with ease, meet deadlines, manage projects, and consistently deliver results. You have gained respect, maybe earned a few promotions, and feel confident in your work. But here is the hidden trap: mastery does not always equal growth. In fact, it can often be the very thing that holds you back.

I have been there. I once found myself in a role that, by all measures, I had mastered. My projects were delivered flawlessly, my team was happy, and I had the trust of senior leadership. From the outside, it looked like I was on the fast track. But inside, I felt this nagging sense of stillness. I was no longer challenged and no longer excited by the work. It took me a while to realize it, but I had hit the invisible ceiling of comfort.

The Comfort Zone Dilemma

I will share a personal story to make this real. A few years ago, I found myself in what seemed like an ideal job. I had been in the role for several years and knew the team and processes like the back of my hand. My day was so predictable that I could operate on autopilot. Challenges were minimal, and I was in good standing with management. Yet, I felt stuck.

That is when it hit me—I was in a comfort zone so deep that I had stopped growing. I was efficient but uninspired, productive but stagnant. And while it felt safe, deep down, I knew I was not evolving. It was not until I started taking risks—like volunteering for projects outside my expertise and offering to support my boss on more strategic tasks—that I began to push past my boundaries.

It was not easy. I made mistakes, lots of them. But those uncomfortable experiences forced me to grow. I began to see myself in a new light, as someone who was not afraid to take on challenges that stretched my abilities. The more I pushed myself, the more visible I became to leadership. New opportunities opened up, and my career trajectory began to shift.

The Invisible Ceiling of Comfort

The comfort zone can be dangerous. When you are too comfortable, you assume you are doing everything right. But that is when growth stalls. You stop pushing your limits, stop seeking new challenges, and unknowingly start coasting. You might think you are waiting for the next promotion or opportunity, but in reality, you could be waiting in vain.

I have seen this pattern in other leaders too. Take Akio Toyoda, former CEO of Toyota, as an example. When he took over, Toyota faced significant challenges, including criticism for being too traditional and a lack of agility in adopting new trends like electric and autonomous vehicles. Instead of playing it safe, Toyoda pushed the company out of its comfort zone. He championed a culture of innovation, steered the development of eco-friendly technologies like hybrid and hydrogen-powered cars, and redefined Toyota's vision for the future of mobility. It wasn't easy—there were setbacks along the way—but his leadership reinvigorated the organization, proving that stepping out of a comfort zone is critical for growth and transformation.

Ask yourself: are you playing it safe in your role? Have you stopped growing because you are too good at what you do? If the answer is yes, it is time to reassess. Comfort feels good, but it rarely leads to the growth you are striving for.

The Fear of Change vs. The Fear of Stagnation

I get it—stepping into unfamiliar territory is terrifying. You might think, "What if I fail?" But here is a more important question: *What if you stay stagnant?* What is scarier—failing or realizing five years from now that you are exactly where you are today?

Mid-career is a critical time to reflect. Are you simply going through the flow? If so, it is time to take action.

Breaking Free from the Comfort Zone

How do you break free? Start by taking on new challenges, even if they scare you. Volunteer for that high-stakes project, offer to assist your boss with strategic-level tasks, or apply for that position you think you are not quite ready for. Yes, you might stumble. But those stumbles are where the growth happens.

I learned this the hard way, but every time I took a step outside my comfort zone, I saw immediate benefits—not just in terms of career progression but also in how I viewed myself as a leader.

If you want to advance in your career, you must be willing to embrace discomfort. Stretch yourself beyond what is easy and familiar. The career growth you want is just beyond the limits of your comfort zone.

The Shift: Taking Action

So how do you break free from this comfort zone?

1. **Seek New Challenges:**

   Take on initiatives that stretch you, even if they are outside of your usual role. Volunteer for new projects, look for complex problems that need solving, and step into roles that require leadership, even if you are not officially in that position.

2. **Help Your Boss Do His Job:**

   One of the best ways to grow is to start doing the work of the role you want. Begin supporting your boss with tasks at the next level of responsibility. This not only demonstrates your readiness for a bigger role but also increases your visibility.

3. **Network and Seek Mentorship:**

   Connect with people outside your immediate circle—both within and outside of your company. Sometimes opportunities come from unexpected places, and the more visible you are, the more likely you are to be considered for new roles. Ask for feedback, request guidance, and show a willingness to take on more than what your job description entails.

4. **Take Risks:**

Risk is often the quickest path to growth. Apply for the roles you think you are not quite ready for. Ask for responsibilities you do not currently have. Take on work that forces you to learn something new.

As Ginni Rometty, former CEO of IBM, said:

"Growth and comfort do not coexist."

So, I will leave you with a question: *What is one uncomfortable step you can take today to break free from your comfort zone and start growing again?* Take that step, and you might be surprised at the doors it opens.

Taking risks can feel terrifying, especially when you have built a stable career. But true growth happens beyond comfort. Let me share a quick story—Bhavish Aggarwal, co-founder of Ola, took a bold step when he transitioned from working in a traditional job at Microsoft to start his own ride-sharing platform. At the time, the Indian market was dominated by traditional taxis, and the idea of app-based ride-hailing was untested in the country. Despite these challenges, Aggarwal saw the potential to revolutionize urban transportation. His risk paid off, transforming Ola into one of the largest ride-hailing platforms in India. It was not comfort but risk that pushed him to new heights.

I have faced similar moments. In my own journey, staying in my comfort zone led to stagnation. It was not until I began seeking challenges—taking on projects beyond my role—that I experienced real growth.

Whether it is **Elon Musk's** bold move into electric vehicles with Tesla and space exploration with SpaceX or Reed Hastings transforming Netflix into a streaming giant, the lesson is clear: risk is the currency of career acceleration.

Lessons for Mid-Career Professionals

What do these examples have in common? These leaders all reached a point in their careers where they could have continued to do what they were already doing well. But instead, they chose to take calculated risks that accelerated their growth and opened up new possibilities. For mid-career professionals, the lesson is clear: risk-taking is essential for continued growth.

It is easy to become complacent after years of hard work. Still, the most successful professionals are those who step outside of their comfort zone and challenge themselves to think bigger, take on new responsibilities, and tackle problems no one else is willing to face. Taking risks does not mean being reckless—it means seizing opportunities that may come with uncertainty but also great potential for reward.

As you reflect on your career, ask yourself: What challenges could I embrace that might push me to the next level? What risks am I avoiding, and how could taking them open new doors?

So, ask yourself, what risks are you avoiding? What bold moves could unlock your next level?

Now, let's dive into *Practical Steps to Push Beyond Your Comfort Zone for Exponential Growth* and explore tangible ways to break free, and step into your next chapter.

Practical Steps to Push Beyond Your Comfort Zone for Exponential Growth

By the time you have hit mid-career, you have likely mastered the art of comfort. You are good at what you do, you have built a rhythm, and you know your job inside and out. But here is the hard truth: comfort can be the silent enemy of growth. The tech industry, like many others, does not wait for anyone. If you are not pushing yourself, you are slowly getting left behind.

I have been there. Early in my career, I felt I was coasting through a stable role. Everything was under control. But after a while, I realized that the steady pace was not bringing me fulfillment or growth. I had to step outside that comfort zone, take on new challenges, and push beyond the familiar. That leap was both exhilarating and terrifying—and it was the key to my career acceleration.

Leaders like Akio Toyoda and Mary Barra have faced pivotal crossroads in their careers. Toyoda could have remained in his established role at Toyota, maintaining the status quo. Instead, he chose to lead a transformative shift, pushing the company toward eco-friendly innovations like hybrid and hydrogen-powered vehicles—ventures that were risky and far from certain at the time. Mary Barra's journey was equally bold. As the first female CEO of General Motors, she took charge during a period of significant challenges, including the company's bankruptcy and restructuring. Barra steered GM toward electric and autonomous vehicle technologies, positioning the company for future growth. What motivated these leaders to take such risks? A deep belief that true innovation and progress lie beyond the comfort of the familiar.

So, how can *you* take that leap? Let's explore practical steps to push beyond your comfort zone and unlock exponential growth.

1. Set Stretch Goals That Scare You

If your current job no longer challenges you, it is time to set stretch goals—targets that feel just a bit out of reach. Think about this: What is something in your role that makes you nervous? Maybe it is leading a cross-functional team or spearheading a project that requires skills you have only dabbled in. It is these goals that push you to evolve, forcing you to grow in ways that safe, routine work never will. For me, stepping into leadership roles before I thought I was ready was my stretch. It was scary but necessary.

Ask Yourself: What project or goal have you been putting off because it seems too ambitious?

2. Volunteer for High-Visibility Projects

Stepping into the spotlight can be nerve-wracking, but these high-stakes projects are the ones that get you noticed. When I took on a project that involved presenting to senior executives, I felt vulnerable. But that visibility opened doors I had not even known existed. Similarly, leaders like Akio Toyoda sought out game-changing projects, such as championing Toyota's pivot toward sustainability with hybrid and hydrogen-powered vehicles—ventures that were bold and aligned with the company's future.

Yes, there's a risk of failure, but the potential upside—being seen as a problem-solver and leader—is worth it. Remember, discomfort is where growth happens.

Ask Yourself: What high-visibility opportunity can you seize, even if it feels intimidating?

3. Embrace Learning—Even When It is Uncomfortable

It is easy to stick to what you know. But when was the last time you learned something completely new? Leaders who thrive are always learning. Think about Reed Hastings from Netflix. His decision to pivot from DVDs to streaming was not based on what was comfortable—it was driven by his constant desire to adapt and grow.

For me, learning new management and technical skills outside my immediate role felt awkward at first. But it gave me a broader perspective, making me more adaptable and valuable.

Ask Yourself: What skill outside your current expertise would push you out of your comfort zone?

4. Get Candid Feedback—Even When It Hurts

Feedback can sting, but it is essential for growth. I used to shy away from feedback, especially when it was critical. But over time, I have come to realize that it is those uncomfortable truths that have helped me grow the most. Leaders like Sheryl Sandberg have often emphasized the importance of seeking out honest feedback as a way to constantly improve.

It is not easy to hear where you might be falling short, but it is necessary. Candid feedback can be the roadmap you need to break through your current barriers.

Ask Yourself: When was the last time you asked for real, no-holds-barred feedback on your leadership or technical skills?

5. Take Calculated Risks

Career growth rarely happens without taking risks. Whether it is switching industries, moving to a leadership role, or leaving a stable job to pursue something unproven, calculated risks are where real growth lies. I remember the internal struggle I felt when considering a leadership position I did not feel ready for. But it was only by stepping into that unknown that I unlocked new opportunities.

Leaders like Reed Hastings built Netflix by risking its entire business model, moving from DVDs to streaming. The risk? Enormous. The reward? Industry-changing.

Ask Yourself: What risk are you avoiding, and how could taking the risk lead to new growth opportunities?

6. Get Comfortable with Discomfort

Here is the truth: nothing transformational happens in your comfort zone. If you are not a little nervous about the challenges ahead, you are likely not pushing yourself hard enough. Industry leaders always step into areas where they are not experts because that is where they learn the most.

For me, learning to sit in discomfort, whether it was tackling new leadership roles or diving into complex projects, was the key to exponential growth.

Ask Yourself: How can you get comfortable with discomfort and start seeing it as a sign of growth?

7. Build a Support Network

Growth does not happen alone. Having mentors and peers who challenge and support you can make all the difference. Leaders like Sandberg did not grow in isolation – they leaned on their networks for feedback and guidance.

Build a circle of people who inspire you to push harder and lean on them when you feel the weight of the challenges you have taken on.

Ask Yourself: Who in your network can help you grow, and who challenges you to push beyond your limits?

Conclusion:

Pushing beyond your comfort zone is not easy, but it is necessary. It is where exponential growth happens, personally and professionally. The question is: Are you ready to embrace the discomfort and leap into something greater?

In the next chapter, we'll dive into *Overcoming Setbacks and Building Resilience*—because with every risk comes the possibility of failure. And that is okay. What matters is how we bounce back. Let's explore the strategies that will help you stay resilient, no matter what challenges come your way.

Chapter 9

Overcoming Setbacks and Building Resilience

Embracing career failures and learning from them.

The Power of Positive Thinking to Energize Your Journey

Strategies for recovering from career setbacks.

How to build resilience and stay focused in challenging environments.

- "Have you ever faced a career setback that felt like a dead end but turned out to be a new beginning? How can seeing failures this way help you succeed?"

- "When you encounter career challenges, do you see them as roadblocks or chances to grow? How can changing your view on setbacks make you more resilient and advance your career?"

Embracing Career Failures and Learning from Them

Embracing Setbacks: A Path to Growth

Experiencing setbacks in your professional life can feel like a punch to the gut. Perhaps you have waited patiently for that promotion that always seems just out of reach. Or maybe you've interviewed for a global role, only to hear the dreaded words, "We're going in a different direction." These moments can shake your confidence and make you question your abilities and direction. It is natural to feel overwhelmed when it seems like your dreams are slipping away. But here is the truth: these challenges are not the end of your journey; they are pivotal moments that can lead to profound growth.

The Reality of Setbacks

Many of us face stagnation or disappointment, especially in our mid-career stages. Think of Steve Jobs, who was ousted from Apple, the company he co-founded. Instead of letting that setback define him, he channeled it into creating NeXT and Pixar, ultimately returning to Apple with new perspectives and innovations that revolutionized the tech industry. His journey exemplifies how career failures can pave the way for future triumphs when approached with resilience and a growth mindset.

Amitabh Bachchan's story is a remarkable example of resilience. Early in his career, he faced numerous rejections, including being dismissed by All India Radio for having an unsuitable voice for broadcasting. Despite these early setbacks, Bachchan's unwavering determination and belief in his potential propelled him forward. He transformed each rejection into motivation, ultimately becoming one of the most influential actors in Indian cinema. His journey is a testament to how embracing failure and persevering through adversity can lead to extraordinary success, reshaping one's career and legacy.

My Own Journey of Setbacks

Like many of you, I have faced both personal challenges and professional roadblocks that seemed impossible to overcome. Mid-career often brings with it a unique set of struggles, and my journey has been no exception.

At a pivotal point in my career, I was on a long-term assignment in the U.S. with my wife and son. A promising opportunity for a permanent role with a competitive salary presented itself—a dream come true for many. But life had other plans. During that time, my extended family had a severe medical emergency in India. Without a second thought, I packed up overnight and returned, leaving behind what could have been a transformative career opportunity. For me, taking care of family is more important than anything else as something can't wait while others can do it.

Professionally, the road was not any easier. For years, promotions felt just out of reach, no matter how hard I worked or how much effort I put in. My aspirations of securing a global role within my company often ended in bitter disappointment. Each failed salary negotiation left me disheartened, as though the dreams I had worked so tirelessly for were slipping further and further away.

These setbacks tested not just my career resilience but also my emotional strength. Yet, they also shaped me into the person I am today—a person who understands the power of persistence, the value of priorities, and the strength it takes to rise again.

Learning from Failure

Embracing failure is not just about acceptance; it is about shifting your perspective. Setbacks are opportunities for growth. After each disappointment, I took time to reflect on what went wrong. I learned to seek feedback and identify areas where I could improve my skills. This reflective practice not only helped me set new goals but also reignited my passion for growth.

Consider the words of Richard Branson, founder of the Virgin Group, who has faced many failed ventures. He advises us to learn from each failure and keep moving forward. Finding a mentor who has navigated similar challenges can provide invaluable guidance and support as you chart your own path.

Building Resilience

Resilience is the cornerstone of overcoming setbacks. It is about developing a mindset that allows you to bounce back stronger than before. One way to build resilience is to cultivate a growth mindset. As Carol Dweck, a renowned psychologist, notes, individuals with a growth mindset view challenges as opportunities rather than threats. This perspective fuels persistence, ultimately leading to success.

Additionally, it is crucial to surround yourself with a supportive network. Lean on colleagues, friends, or professional groups who can offer encouragement during tough times. Sheryl Sandberg, Facebook's COO, has openly discussed how her support network helped her navigate personal and professional challenges.

Embracing the Journey Ahead

Ultimately, embracing career failures means recognizing that setbacks are a natural part of our professional journey. They do not define our worth; rather, they refine our paths and build our resilience. As Nelson Mandela wisely said, **"I never lose. I either win or learn."** This mindset is essential in transforming setbacks into stepping stones toward future success.

As you navigate your next challenge, remember that this is not the end; it is a new beginning. Embrace the lessons, seek growth, think positively, and build resilience. Your journey through setbacks will not only shape your career but also foster personal growth.

The Power of Positive Thinking in Mid-Career: Energizing Your Journey

Mid-career is a pivotal phase—a time when you have built a foundation yet strive to reach higher peaks. It is also a time rife with challenges: missed promotions, shifting priorities, and the ever-looming question of "What's next?" Your mindset becomes your compass, steering your journey through the highs and lows.

Negative thinking often creeps in during tough times. It is natural to feel disheartened when progress feels stagnant or goals seem elusive. I have experienced it myself, whether it was dealing with a long-awaited promotion slipping away or grappling with the fear of being left behind in a rapidly evolving industry. Negative thoughts act like quicksand, pulling you into doubt and limiting your ability to see solutions. Professionally, they can narrow your perspective, stifling creativity and confidence. Personally, they can spill over into your family life, creating unnecessary tension and stress.

Take the story of Michael Jordan, one of the greatest basketball players of all time. Early in his career, Jordan faced setbacks, including being cut from his high school basketball team. Instead of succumbing to negativity, he channeled his disappointment into relentless practice and self-belief.

Jordan famously said, *"I have failed over and over and over again in my life, and that is why I succeed."* His ability to turn failure into fuel for growth exemplifies the transformative power of positive thinking.

But positive thinking is not about blind optimism. It is about building resilience, adopting a solution-oriented mindset, and focusing on opportunities rather than obstacles. When you approach challenges with positivity, you do not just survive—you thrive.

Consider the teachings of Swami Vivekananda, whose philosophy on the power of thought remains timeless. He emphasized, *"We are what our thoughts have made us; so take care of what you think."* Swami Vivekananda inspired millions by advocating for a strong, positive mindset as the foundation for personal and collective growth. His life stands as a testament to the power of inner strength and unwavering belief in one's potential, even in the face of adversity.

How to Shift Your Thinking

So, how can you cultivate a positive mindset, especially when faced with difficulties? Here are some strategies to help you lead with resilience and optimism:

1. **Pause and Reframe**

   When you catch yourself in a cycle of negative thoughts, pause. Ask yourself: *"Is this thought helping or holding me back?"* Shift your focus from what's wrong to what can be done. For example, instead of saying, "Why does this always happen to me?" try asking, "What lesson can I learn here?"

2. **Celebrate Small Wins**

   Big goals can feel overwhelming. Break them down into smaller, manageable steps and celebrate each milestone.

As Jeff Bezos says, *"Success is never about one big breakthrough. It is about countless small improvements."* Focusing on progress, no matter how small, fuels motivation and builds momentum.

3. Practice Gratitude

Start your day with a gratitude ritual. Reflect on three things you're thankful for, whether it is a supportive colleague, a lesson learned, or even the opportunity to try again. Gratitude shifts your perspective and brings positive energy into your day.

4. Surround Yourself with Positivity

Jim Rohn famously said, *"You are the average of the five people you spend the most time with."* Surround yourself with people who inspire and uplift you. Engage in conversations and activities that fuel your growth and energize your mindset.

5. Control the Controllable

As a mid-career professional, there will always be elements beyond your control—industry trends, team dynamics, or organizational changes. Focus on what you can control: your skills, your attitude, and your actions. This clarity will help you navigate challenges with confidence.

The Balance Between Realism and Optimism

Positive thinking does not mean ignoring reality. Acknowledging negative emotions is important—they serve as signals that something needs attention. For example, if you feel undervalued at work, suppressing those feelings will not help. Instead, channel that energy into productive actions: seeking feedback, upskilling, or exploring new roles.

Consider the example of Dr. A.P.J. Abdul Kalam during the early stages of India's space program. When the first Satellite Launch Vehicle (SLV) mission failed in 1979, Dr. Kalam, who was the project director, faced immense pressure and disappointment. However, he did not allow this setback to define his career or the team's future. Instead, he analyzed the failure, reassessed strategies, and worked tirelessly with his team to achieve success in the next launch in 1980. This resilience and ability to maintain optimism under extreme adversity made him one of the most respected leaders in history. As Dr. Kalam said, *"Man needs difficulties in life because they are necessary to enjoy success."*

Energizing Your Personal and Professional Life

The effects of a positive mindset ripple through every aspect of your life. Professionally, it fuels innovation and strengthens your ability to lead and inspire others. Personally, it enhances your relationships and emotional well-being. When you approach situations with optimism, you create an environment where growth thrives—for yourself and those around you.

Remember, positivity is a choice. Every day, you have the power to shape your thoughts, actions, and ultimately, your destiny. As you move forward in your mid-career journey, ask yourself: *"What kind of energy am I creating today?"* Choose the energy that lifts you, empowers you, and sets you on the path to success. You have the tools to lead with resilience, optimism, and impact. Now, go out there and rise.

Now, let's explore some **strategies for recovering from career setbacks** that will empower you to Rise and Lead stronger than ever.

Strategies for Recovering from Career Setbacks

Setbacks in our careers can feel like insurmountable walls, leaving us disheartened and questioning our worth. I have faced my share of challenges—those prolonged waits for a promotion, the global roles that slipped through my fingers, and salary negotiations that stalled without clear answers. Each setback felt like a personal blow, but I learned that how we respond to these obstacles can redefine our paths forward.

1. Take Action and Address Your Gaps

After facing a setback, the first step is often to take a hard look at what contributed to that experience. What gaps can you address? Reflect on feedback and identify the skills or experiences that need bolstering. For instance, after missing out on a promotion, I took it upon myself to seek out mentorship and training in areas where I felt inadequate. This proactive approach not only made me a more competitive candidate but also reignited my confidence.

Example: Think of Howard Schultz, the former CEO of Starbucks. Faced with countless rejections while trying to expand Starbucks from a local coffee shop to a global powerhouse, Schultz did not let failure deter him. He took action by refining his business strategies and focusing on crafting a unique customer experience, ultimately leading to Starbucks' worldwide acclaim.

> **"Success is not final, failure is not fatal.
> It is the courage to continue that counts."**
> — Winston Churchill

2. Prepare for the Next Big Opportunity

Getting ready for your next big opportunity involves more than simply addressing gaps; it requires strategic planning. Are you looking to transition to a different business unit or organization? Develop a clear action plan, set goals, and take steps towards them. For me, this meant updating my resume, networking within the industry, and identifying roles that aligned with my aspirations.

Example: When Jensen Huang co-founded NVIDIA and later steered it as CEO, he faced significant challenges in a highly competitive semiconductor industry. Huang's preparation involved identifying the untapped potential of GPU technology and setting a bold vision for its applications beyond gaming, including AI and data centers. His strategic planning transformed NVIDIA into a market leader, revolutionizing industries with groundbreaking innovations in AI and high-performance computing.

> **"By failing to prepare, you are preparing to fail."**
> — Benjamin Franklin

3. Expand Your Horizons

Expanding your knowledge is vital. Exploring new industries, technologies, or skills can uncover unexpected opportunities.

Embrace continuous learning; it is the key to staying relevant and adaptable in today's fast-paced job market.

During my own setbacks, I committed to learning about emerging fields and trends. This broadened my perspective and enhanced my versatility, making me more appealing to potential employers.

Example: Consider Elon Musk, founder of SpaceX and Tesla. With no formal training in rocket science, Musk immersed himself in learning. His relentless pursuit of knowledge led to groundbreaking innovations across multiple industries.

"The only way to do great work is to love what you do."
— Steve Jobs

4. Embrace Abundant Opportunities

In the face of setbacks, it is crucial to recognize that opportunities abound. Each challenge carries the seeds of potential growth. By maintaining an optimistic mindset, you can turn obstacles into stepping stones.

In my own journey, optimism kept me motivated despite setbacks. I learned to view challenges as opportunities for growth, leading me to identify new paths and avenues for advancement.

Example: J.K. Rowling faced countless rejections before publishing her first Harry Potter book. Yet, she held steadfast to her belief in her story, ultimately leading to her monumental success.

"The best way to predict the future is to create it."
— Peter Drucker

Key Note:

Recovering from career setbacks is about taking proactive steps, preparing strategically, expanding your knowledge, and embracing opportunities. These strategies transform challenges into avenues for growth and success. Remember, setbacks are not dead ends but are parts of your journey towards achieving your goals.

As we move forward, let's explore **Building Resilience and Staying Focused in Challenging Environments**, ensuring we equip ourselves with the tools necessary to thrive amidst adversity.

Building Resilience and Staying Focused in Challenging Environments.

In the midst of career setbacks, building resilience and maintaining focus is crucial for navigating through adversity and emerging stronger. Resilience is not just about bouncing back from challenges but about growing and evolving through them. As someone who has faced significant professional obstacles—such as prolonged periods without promotion, missed global opportunities and stalled salary negotiations—I have learned firsthand the importance of resilience and focus. My journey, coupled with industry examples, illustrates how embracing a systematic approach can help you build resilience and stay focused.

The Journey of Building Resilience

My own experience with setbacks taught me valuable lessons about resilience. Confronted with a lack of promotion and unsuccessful attempts at securing a global role, I initially felt daunted and pressured. These challenges led me to confront my limited beliefs and overcome my fear of failure. I realized that to build a strong foundation for my future, I needed to explore new avenues, such as mentorship, and prepare myself for the next set of challenges. This journey towards resilience involved a strategic framework called the **"CARE" Framework**: **C**larity, **A**ction, **R**eflection, and **E**ndurance. This framework guided me through tough times and can serve as a powerful tool for others facing similar challenges.

1. Clarity: Define Your Goals and Values

The first step in building resilience is gaining clarity about your goals and values. Understanding what you want to achieve and why it matters to you provides a sense of purpose and direction, even in the face of setbacks. When faced with career stagnation, I took time to reflect on my long-term aspirations and values. This clarity helped me focus on what was truly important and allowed me to navigate challenges with a renewed sense of purpose.

Example: Consider Jeff Bezos, the founder of Amazon. Early in his career, Bezos faced numerous challenges and skepticism about his vision for an online bookstore. Despite the obstacles, his clarity about his goal—to build a customer-centric company—kept him focused. This clear vision enabled him to persevere and ultimately transform Amazon into a global e-commerce giant.

2. Action: Take Proactive Steps.

Building resilience requires taking proactive actions to address your challenges and prepare for future opportunities. In my case, I focused on addressing my skill gaps, seeking mentorship, and exploring new areas of interest. These actions not only helped me stay engaged but also positioned me better for new opportunities.

Example: Elon Musk's journey is a prime example of taking proactive action. Musk faced numerous setbacks in his ventures, including the early struggles of SpaceX and Tesla. Instead of succumbing to these challenges, he took decisive actions to address issues, such as investing in new technologies and scaling operations. His proactive approach played a significant role in overcoming obstacles and achieving remarkable success.

"You miss 100% of the shots you don't take."
— Wayne Gretzky.

3. Reflection: Learn and Adapt

Reflection is a crucial component of resilience. Taking time to analyze your experiences and learn from them helps you adapt and improve. After experiencing setbacks, I engaged in reflective practices, such as evaluating feedback and identifying areas for growth. This process of reflection enabled me to adapt my strategies and enhance my approach.

Example: J.K. Rowling, author of the Harry Potter series, faced numerous rejections before finding a publisher. Through reflection and perseverance, she refined her manuscript and approach. Her ability to learn from feedback and adapt her strategies ultimately led to one of the most successful literary franchises in history.

"The measure of intelligence is the ability to change."
— Albert Einstein

4. Endurance: Stay Committed and Persistent.

Endurance is about maintaining commitment and persistence, even when facing ongoing challenges. Building resilience involves staying focused and continuing to move forward despite setbacks. Throughout my career, maintaining endurance meant pushing through tough times and remaining committed to my goals, no matter how difficult the journey seemed.

Example: Oprah Winfrey's career is a testament to endurance. Despite facing numerous setbacks and personal challenges, Winfrey remained committed to her vision and continued to push forward. Her perseverance through adversity played a crucial role in her success as a media mogul and philanthropist.

> "It does not matter how slowly you go
> as long as you do not stop."
> — Confucius

Conclusion

Building resilience in challenging environments requires a clear roadmap—let's call it the "CARE" Framework: Clarity, Action, Reflection, and Endurance. Imagine you are facing a career setback; gaining clarity about your goals becomes crucial. For instance, when I felt stalled in my career, I set specific goals to guide my actions.

Next, take proactive steps. Like Howard Schultz, who transformed Starbucks through persistent action, we must address our gaps and seek growth. Reflect on your experiences; J.K. Rowling faced numerous rejections yet learned from each, ultimately shaping her success.

Finally, endurance is vital. As Nelson Mandela said, "It always seems impossible until it's done." Embrace each challenge as an opportunity, knowing your resilience can lead to long-term success and organizational impact. Now, let's explore how this resilience translates into lasting achievements in your career.

Part 5

Long-Term Success and Organizational Impact

Chapter 10

Leading Organizational Transformation

How to influence positive change in your organization.

Fostering a culture of excellence and continuous improvement.

Practical strategies for driving innovation and organizational growth

"What if real change in your organization didn't need a big overhaul but started with small steps? How can you lead that change?"

"Is your organization growing or just getting by? What would it take to create a culture where excellence and innovation lead to long-term success?"

Leading Positive Change: A Journey of Empowerment and Growth

As I reflect on my journey of creating a Center of Excellence (CoE) in one of the site in my previous organization, I am reminded of the profound impact that leadership can have on fostering a positive and high-energy work environment. It was not just about meeting deadlines or hitting targets; it was about creating a space where every team member felt empowered, motivated, and connected to a shared purpose.

The Role of Leadership in Driving Positive Change

Positive change begins at the leadership level, but it must permeate every layer of the organization. As leaders, our role is not just to manage timelines and budgets, but to ensure that our organization thrives, surpasses expectations, and fosters a culture of excellence that competes on the global stage.

When I led the CoE, I realized that our success was not just about efficiency; it was about instilling a sense of ownership and creating an energized workplace. I remember one team member who was hesitant to take on new responsibilities. By giving him the freedom to explore new ideas without fear of failure, he blossomed into one of our most innovative thinkers. This was not just about his growth; it was about creating an environment where everyone felt valued and supported.

Creating a Culture of Empowerment and Exploration

Empowering your team members is crucial for driving positive change. When people feel valued, heard, and supported, they are more likely to take initiative and step out of their comfort zones. But this requires a mindset shift—from focusing solely on deliverables to prioritizing people and culture.

I recall a project where we faced significant setbacks. Instead of pointing fingers or punishing failure, we asked ourselves: "What can we learn from this?" This simple question transformed our approach from one of blame to one of continuous learning. We celebrated failures as stepping stones to success, fostering a culture where experimentation was encouraged and learning was constant.

Showing Gratitude and Recognition.

Appreciation is often overlooked but is a powerful tool for motivating and energizing an organization. Recognizing achievements—both big and small—deepens employees' sense of belonging and purpose.

In the CoE, celebrating every success became part of our culture. I encouraged leaders at every level to show appreciation regularly—whether through formal recognition programs or simply acknowledging a job well done. One team member told me how much it meant to her when her manager acknowledged her hard work during a team meeting. It made her feel seen and valued.

This focus on gratitude created an environment where positivity flourished. People were more inclined to take ownership of their work because they knew their contributions were valued.

Building Trust and Global Credibility

Positive change is not just internal; it is also about building trust with external stakeholders. When leading the CoE, building strong relationships with other global teams was essential.

I spent a significant amount of time ensuring everyone felt included in our mission through constant communication and cross-functional collaboration. By involving everyone in key initiatives, we built trust that extended beyond our immediate team.

This trust-building effort was not just symbolic; it was crucial for our survival and success. The more we involved our global counterparts and demonstrated our commitment to excellence, the more they trusted us with critical projects.

Driving a Positive Work Environment.

Influencing positive change requires a holistic approach that goes beyond operational efficiency. It requires leaders to focus on people—creating an environment where energy, empowerment, and trust are at the core.

As I look back on my journey with the CoE, I realize that it is about constantly enabling opportunities for growth, rewarding people for their efforts, showing gratitude, and maintaining a positive environment free from toxicity.

Fostering a Culture of Excellence and Continuous Improvement

So, how do we take this positive change to the next level? How do we foster a culture of excellence and continuous improvement?

The answer lies in creating an organization where every individual feels empowered to contribute and excel. It is about setting up systems that encourage continuous learning, innovation, and collaboration.

In my next chapter, I will delve deeper into how you can foster this culture within your own organization. We'll explore practical strategies for embedding excellence into every aspect of your work—from setting clear goals aligned with your mission to creating feedback loops that drive continuous improvement.

Together, let's build organizations that are not just functioning but flourishing—an environment where every team member feels empowered to contribute meaningfully while driving both personal and organizational growth.

By focusing on these core principles—empowerment, gratitude, and trust-building—you can become the driving force for positive change in your organization. Remember: it is not just about what you achieve; it is about how you make your team feel along the way. Let's embark on this journey together towards fostering cultures of excellence that thrive in every aspect.

Fostering a Culture of Excellence and Continuous Improvement: A Personal Journey

As I reflect on my career, particularly the time I led a Center of Excellence (CoE), I am reminded of the transformative power of fostering a culture of excellence and continuous improvement. This journey was not just about achieving organizational success; it was about personal growth, empowerment, and creating an environment where everyone thrived.

The Power of Gamification

One of the most engaging ways to foster this culture is through gamification. I remember introducing gamification into our daily work routines, and it was like a spark had been lit. Routine tasks became competitive and engaging, tapping into people's natural desire for competition, recognition, and reward. Our teams were motivated to improve in every aspect of their work—from writing better requirements to implementing code with fewer errors.

I recall one team member who was initially hesitant but soon found himself competing with colleagues to share best practices and adopt Agile and Lean principles. This was not just about individual success; it was about creating a collective culture of improvement. As more people engaged, our productivity soared, cycle times shrank, and efficiency improved dramatically.

Excellence in Everyday Work

Excellence is not just about grand initiatives; it is about excelling in everyday tasks. When we implemented this mindset in our CoE, we encouraged team members to take ownership of their work and constantly look for ways to improve. Whether it was refining a report or enhancing customer interactions, every interaction presented an opportunity to do better.

I remember a young analyst who took it upon himself to streamline our reporting process. His small improvements might have seemed insignificant at first but collectively made a significant impact on our efficiency. This empowered mindset created a ripple effect throughout the organization, where improvement became second nature.

Embracing Kaizen and Agile Principles

We embraced Agile and Lean principles, focusing on Kaizen—the practice of continuous, incremental improvement. Kaizen became a core part of our culture, where everyone had the opportunity to bring forth new ideas. Even the smallest improvements were celebrated because they contributed to moving us from our current state to the next level.

I recall a team meeting where an intern suggested a minor tweak in our coding process that ended up reducing errors by 20%. This small victory was celebrated across the board because it exemplified our commitment to continuous improvement.

Servant Leadership: Empowering Your Team

For a culture of excellence to thrive, you need more than processes—you need the right mindset and leadership style. Servant leadership was instrumental in our success. As leaders, our role shifted from taskmasters to mentors and enablers.

When I adopted this approach, I saw teams interact differently. Leaders worked alongside team members, breaking down barriers and removing obstacles. This style encouraged open communication, trust, and collaboration. Teams felt empowered because they knew they had the support of their leaders.

Strategic Planning and Value Stream Mapping

To foster a culture of excellence, you must think strategically and plan for the long-term. We implemented a Strategic Development Plan that aligned our day-to-day work with long-term goals. By revisiting this plan monthly, we ensured we were always moving towards our vision.

Value Stream Mapping was another invaluable tool. It helped us visualize where we were spending time and resources and identify areas for improvement. This process uncovered hidden bottlenecks and made our workflows more efficient.

Learning from Industry Leaders

Industry leaders like Toyota and Amazon have shown us how a focus on continuous improvement can transform organizations. Toyota's commitment to lean manufacturing and Kaizen has allowed them to maintain a competitive edge for decades. Amazon's willingness to experiment, learn from failures, and refine processes has kept them at the forefront of innovation.

Excellence as a Way of Life

At the heart of this culture is the mindset that there is always room for growth, always something new to learn. This mindset can transform not only organizations but also individuals within them.

For mid-career professionals navigating uncertainty or seeking revitalization in their careers, embracing this culture can be transformative. It opens doors to new opportunities and provides the energy and focus needed to rise again.

As Brian Tracy once said, **"Excellence is not a destination; it is a continuous journey that never ends."** By committing to continuous improvement—by pushing yourself and your team every day—you create an environment where excellence becomes second nature.

Driving Innovation and Organizational Growth

As we delve into fostering a culture of excellence and continuous improvement, it becomes clear that this journey is just the beginning. The next step is driving innovation and organizational growth—a topic we will explore in depth next.

Imagine an organization where every member feels empowered not just to improve processes but also to innovate boldly, where failure is seen as part of the learning process rather than a setback. Where strategic planning meets creative thinking.

In our next topic, we'll explore practical strategies for driving innovation, including how to leverage design thinking and encourage intrapreneurship within your organization.

Practical Strategies for Driving Innovation and Organizational Growth

In today's fast-paced world, innovation is the spark that ignites organizational growth and propels careers forward. As a mid-career professional, embracing innovation can be a game-changer, both personally and professionally. But fostering a culture of innovation does not happen overnight; it requires deliberate strategies, visionary leadership, and an environment that encourages creative thinking.

The Power of Strategic Development Plans

One of the most effective tools I have used to drive innovation is the Strategic Development Plan (SDP). This is not just a high-level roadmap; it is a living document that provides the structure and focus needed to innovate. By revisiting this plan monthly, you can realign your efforts with long-term goals and identify new opportunities for innovation.

I remember when we first implemented our SDP in our Center of Excellence. It was like giving our team a North Star to guide them. We would meet monthly to review progress, celebrate successes, and identify areas where we could innovate further. This process gave us clarity and direction, allowing us to push the boundaries of what was possible.

Inspiring Innovation Through Real-World Examples

Strategic planning is crucial, but it is not enough on its own. As a leader, your role is to inspire your team to think innovatively. I have found that sharing real-world examples of industry-specific innovations can be incredibly powerful. When I shared stories of how companies like Apple or Tesla used breakthrough innovations to leapfrog competitors, it sparked a vision in my team of what was achievable.

For instance, I recall a team meeting where we discussed how Tesla's innovative approach to electric vehicles transformed the automotive industry. This discussion motivated my team to think beyond their current scope of work and explore how their unique skills could contribute to larger organizational growth.

Innovation Beyond Products

Innovation is not just about products; it is about processes, people, and perspectives. Even if your team is not working on groundbreaking technology, they can still innovate in how they approach problem-solving or streamline workflows. These small innovations can accumulate, leading to significant improvements in efficiency and productivity.

I saw this firsthand when one of our teams introduced a new mistake-proofing methodology that reduced errors by 30%. This was not a revolutionary product innovation but a process improvement that had a profound impact on our overall quality.

Empowering Teams to Experiment

To foster an innovative environment, you must give teams the freedom to experiment. This means providing opportunities to explore new ideas, take calculated risks, and even fail—because failure is often the seed of innovation. When teams feel empowered to step out of their comfort zones without fear of repercussions, they are more likely to engage in creative problem-solving.

I remember a young developer who was hesitant to suggest a new approach because he feared it might not work. But when we created an environment where experimentation was encouraged, he felt confident enough to propose his idea. Although it did not work as planned initially, it led to a breakthrough that improved our coding efficiency significantly.

Providing Resources and Support

Leaders must also provide the necessary resources and support for innovation. Whether it is training on emerging technologies, dedicating time to innovation sprints, or providing access to industry research, giving teams the tools they need can unlock new possibilities.

For example, many organizations have embraced hackathons or innovation labs where teams can collaborate on developing new ideas in a pressure-free environment. I have seen these events spark some of the most innovative solutions within our organization.

Building a Collaborative Ecosystem

Driving innovation is not just about individual contributions; it is about creating a collaborative ecosystem. Sharing best practices across teams, departments, and even external partners creates a knowledge-sharing culture where innovation thrives.

I recall a cross-functional project in which our marketing, sales, service and development teams collaborated to develop a new product feature. The diverse perspectives brought to the table resulted in an innovative solution that exceeded our expectations.

The Fulfilling Experience of Championing Innovation

As mid-career professionals, championing innovation can be an incredibly fulfilling experience. It reinvigorates your career by pushing you out of your comfort zone and positions you as a leader who drives organizational growth.

Remember Steve Jobs's words: **"Innovation distinguishes between a leader and a follower."**

By fostering innovation within your team, you contribute to the sustained excellence and evolution of your entire organization.

Segway to Future-Proofing Your Career

As we explore these practical strategies for driving innovation and organizational growth, it becomes clear that this journey is closely tied to future-proofing your career.

Imagine being at the forefront of industry trends, equipped with the skills and mindset to adapt to any change. By understanding how to drive innovation today, you will be better prepared to navigate tomorrow's challenges and opportunities. Let's move forward together on this journey towards future-proofing your career and long-term success.

Framework: ACT: Align Vision and Values, Cultivate Collaboration, Trigger Action and Accountability - A Framework for Leading Change

1. **A - Align Vision and Values** To drive positive change in any organization, alignment between the organization's vision and its values is crucial. Mid-career professionals must ensure that their personal goals align with the company's mission and culture. Without alignment, efforts to inspire change may feel disjointed or superficial. Whether it is building a new team or leading an organizational shift, clear communication of a shared vision helps employees understand the "why" behind the change. As a leader, take time to align goals across departments and ensure that every team member sees how their work contributes to the bigger picture. **Alignment creates momentum.**

2. **C - Cultivate Collaboration** is the foundation of innovation and growth. Leaders at the mid-career level should foster an environment where collaboration is not only

encouraged but expected. By breaking down silos between teams and departments, leaders can create open channels for idea-sharing and problem-solving. Embrace cross-functional teams and ensure that diverse perspectives are heard and valued. When employees collaborate on meaningful projects, they take ownership of their contributions, which in turn fuels innovation and continuous improvement. **Collaboration builds trust and drives results.**

3. **T - Trigger Action and Accountability** Positive change cannot happen without action. It is easy to talk about improvement, but change leaders must trigger actionable steps that employees can take to contribute to transformation. Begin by identifying the key areas where immediate impact is needed, and set clear, measurable goals. Encourage employees to take ownership of their roles, making them accountable for specific outcomes. Celebrate small wins along the way, as these victories motivate the team to continue pushing boundaries. **Action turns strategy into reality, while accountability ensures long-term success.**

GROW: Goal-Setting, Resilience, Ownership, Workforce Development -Framework for Sustainable Organizational Excellence

1. **G - Goal-Setting** Establishing clear, long-term goals is the cornerstone of sustainable growth. These goals should be ambitious but attainable, giving the organization a clear

direction for the future. For mid-career professionals, it is vital to ensure that these goals reflect both personal career aspirations and broader organizational needs. Set key performance indicators (KPIs) and track progress regularly.

2. **R - Resilience** Change is not always smooth, and setbacks are inevitable. Leaders must foster resilience within teams to ensure they remain adaptable during periods of transformation. Cultivating a mindset where challenges are seen as opportunities for growth helps maintain forward momentum even in difficult times.

3. **O - Ownership** Encourage employees to take ownership of their roles within the organization's transformation journey. When people feel empowered and accountable for their contributions, they are more engaged, creative, and motivated to see projects through. Ownership ensures that change is driven from all levels of the organization.

4. **W - Workforce Development** Investing in employee development is key to driving innovation and continuous improvement. Provide opportunities for learning and growth, whether through formal training or mentorship programs. The more skilled and informed your workforce is, the better equipped they will be to innovate and contribute to the organization's long-term success.

Conclusion

For mid-career professionals looking to lead organizational transformation, frameworks like **ACT** and **GROW** provide actionable steps to drive positive change, foster a culture of excellence, and promote long-term growth. By aligning vision and values, cultivating collaboration, and triggering accountability, leaders can create an environment where innovation and continuous improvement thrive. Additionally, setting ambitious goals, fostering resilience, and promoting workforce development ensure that the organization remains agile and competitive in a rapidly changing marketplace. Ultimately, embracing these strategies positions mid-career professionals not just as contributors to their organizations, but as transformational leaders

Chapter 11

Future-Proofing Your Career for Long-Term Success

Preparing for future challenges in leadership and tech.

Aligning personal growth with future industry trends.

How to build a sustainable, thriving career in the ever-evolving IT industry?

- **With technology changing so quickly, are you ready for the challenges of tomorrow? 3. What if focusing on your personal growth and industry trends could secure your future and make you a leader?4. As industries evolve and leadership roles require new skills, are you prepared to adapt and succeed? Learn how to future-proof your career and stay ahead in the fast-moving IT world."**

Preparing for Future Challenges in Leadership and Tech

In today's whirlwind of technological advancements and constant disruptions, the business landscape is evolving at an unprecedented pace. Industries once dominated by established players are now being challenged by new entrants leveraging the latest technologies and innovative strategies. For mid-career professionals, the message is clear: to stay relevant, you must evolve.

Understanding the Seismic Shifts

The first step in preparing for the future is understanding the profound changes happening in both leadership roles and technology. The rise of AI, Machine Learning (ML), blockchain, cybersecurity, and digital transformation means industries are no longer just looking for "doers" but for leaders who can navigate complexity, drive innovation, and manage multidisciplinary teams.

I recall my own journey when I transitioned from a technical expert to a leadership role. Initially, I was comfortable with my technical skills, but I soon realized that the future demanded more. I had to develop a deep understanding of emerging technologies, strategic thinking, and the ability to foster collaboration across various functions. This was particularly crucial as companies shifted to agile, remote, and hybrid work environments that required new leadership styles.

The Example of Sundar Pichai

Consider Sundar Pichai's journey at Google. Initially hired to lead the Google Toolbar and Chrome efforts. Over the years, he became known for his collaborative leadership style, his deep understanding of Google's technical and business goals, and his ability to navigate internal and external challenges. Today, as CEO of Alphabet, Pichai's leadership is not just about managing teams but about integrating cutting-edge technologies like AI into Google's product roadmap to maintain market leadership.

Adaptation and Continuous Learning

One of the biggest mistakes mid-career professionals make is assuming their existing skills and accomplishments will carry them through to retirement. In reality, the half-life of skills is shrinking rapidly. What may have taken decades to change in previous generations can now shift in a matter of years.

Elon Musk is a prime example of this mindset. Despite already leading two highly innovative companies, Musk continuously educates himself about new industries—whether it is sustainable energy or aerospace—and brings that knowledge back into his businesses. His commitment to learning and evolving is what allows him to stay at the cutting-edge of multiple industries.

For me, this meant enrolling in leadership courses, learning at least a moderate level of AI to apply to real-time projects, and attending industry-specific webinars. The goal was to continuously upskill myself and align with emerging trends.

I remember feeling overwhelmed at first, but each new skill I acquired gave me a sense of confidence and preparedness for the future.

Leveraging Networks and Mentorship

The future of leadership in tech is not just about technical knowledge and innovation; it is also about leveraging networks and finding mentors who can provide guidance and insight. In an industry where roles are rapidly evolving, having the right connections can make all the difference.

Sundar Pichai, the CEO of Google, is a great example of this. When Pichai became CEO, he recognized the importance of continuous learning, both from a technology and a leadership perspective. He credits much of his leadership growth to having the right mentors and his commitment to fostering a culture of collaboration and innovation at Google. Under his guidance, Google has continued to push the boundaries of technology, evolving into a leader in AI and cloud computing while maintaining a strong focus on inclusivity and global impact.

I have found similar value in networking. Joining professional associations, attending industry conferences, and participating in tech meetups have helped me grow my professional network. These connections have provided new perspectives and insights that have been invaluable in my career.

Building a Game Plan for the Future

As technology reshapes industries, mid-career professionals must actively build a game plan to navigate future challenges. Here is a suggested approach:

Identify Skill Gaps: Take a realistic look at your current skill set and identify the gaps that may prevent you from advancing in the future.

Develop a Learning Plan: Create a plan to bridge those gaps. This might include formal education, hands-on learning, or informal learning through books, podcasts, and blogs.

Leverage Your Network: Seek out industry leaders and mentors who can guide your learning journey.

Take Action: The most important step is action. Whether you are exploring new roles, taking on leadership responsibilities, or actively learning new technologies, keep moving forward.

Navigating the Future with Confidence

The journey to future-proofing your career may seem daunting, but it is an opportunity to lead in this fast-changing landscape. By aligning yourself with emerging trends, embracing continuous learning, leveraging your networks, and building a concrete game plan, you can not only survive but thrive in the next phase of your career.

As John F. Kennedy once said, **"Change is the law of life. And those who look only to the past or present are certain to miss the future."** Let this be your motivation as you prepare for the future challenges in leadership and tech—because the future belongs to those who are ready to shape

Aligning Personal Growth with Future Industry Trends

As we stand at the threshold of the fourth industrial revolution, where technologies like AI, Machine Learning (ML), IoT, and blockchain are transforming industries at an unprecedented pace, the key to career success lies in aligning your personal growth with these future trends. For mid-career professionals, this is not just about staying relevant; it is about positioning yourself to lead in this new era.

Adapting to Change in Technology-Driven Industries

Many of us have built our careers on a foundation of specific skills or expertise, often mastering technical or managerial roles over decades. However, in today's fast-evolving world, these skills alone may not suffice for long-term success, especially if you aspire to take on executive roles that shape the direction of an organization.

I recall my own journey when I had to adapt to the shifting landscape of technology. Initially, I was comfortable with my technical skills, but I soon realized that the future demanded more. I had to develop a deep understanding of emerging technologies and strategic thinking to navigate the complexities of our industry.

The Example of a Salesforce Leader

In the tech industry, **Marc Benioff**, the CEO of Salesforce, offers a compelling example. When Benioff founded Salesforce in 1999, he recognized the potential of cloud computing at a time when traditional software models dominated. He was determined to revolutionize the software industry by offering a customer relationship management (CRM) platform that operated entirely in the cloud. By focusing on customer success and innovation, Benioff built Salesforce into a global leader in cloud-based software solutions. His ability to identify and capitalize on emerging trends, while fostering a company culture centered around trust and innovation, highlights the importance of adapting to market shifts and creating long-term success.

Staying Ahead of the Curve: Identifying Key Trends

To align your personal growth with industry trends, you need to identify the technologies driving change in your sector. For tech-based industries, some critical trends include:

Artificial Intelligence (AI) and Machine Learning (ML): From automating customer service to enhancing predictive analytics, AI and ML are redefining how businesses operate.

Blockchain and Decentralization: Blockchain is revolutionizing industries beyond finance, offering transparency, security, and efficiency.

Cybersecurity: As companies digitize their operations, cybersecurity is becoming a boardroom priority.

Cloud Computing: The ability to manage, store, and analyze vast amounts of data has made cloud computing a key trend.

Consider Jeff Bezos's forward-thinking approach at Amazon. Early in Amazon's journey, Bezos identified the shift towards cloud computing and founded AWS, which now accounts for a significant portion of Amazon's revenue. This proactive approach not only ensured Amazon's growth but also established Bezos as a visionary leader.

The Importance of Lifelong Learning

The half-life of skills is shrinking rapidly. What got you to where you are today may not be enough to propel you to the next level. Lifelong learning is essential for mid-career professionals who want to stay ahead.

Mary Barra, the CEO of General Motors, is a prime example. As automotive technology shifted towards electric vehicles and autonomous driving, Barra proactively championed GM's transformation into a leader in these areas. She embraced the learning curve and led the company to align with future trends, ensuring GM remains competitive in a rapidly changing market.

For me, this meant pursuing executive education programs focused on AI and digital transformation, networking with thought leaders, and attending industry conferences to stay updated on cutting-edge developments. It is important not just to stay informed but also to immerse yourself in these new technologies so you can confidently lead teams through the transformations they will inevitably face.

Shifting from Doer to Leader

Mid-career professionals often find themselves at a crossroads where they are no longer just 'doing' the work but are instead stepping into leadership roles that influence strategy, culture, and innovation. To lead effectively in the future, it is essential to move beyond operational roles and take a strategic approach that incorporates future industry trends.

Indra Nooyi's leadership at PepsiCo exemplifies this shift. As CEO, Nooyi saw that consumer preferences were shifting toward healthier options and sustainability. She spearheaded a transformation at PepsiCo that focused on "Performance with Purpose", incorporating healthier products and environmentally friendly practices. Her ability to foresee industry changes and align her leadership approach with those trends ensured PepsiCo's long-term growth and relevance.

Embracing a Growth Mindset

A growth mindset is critical when aligning personal development with future industry trends. Leaders who are adaptable, open to new ideas, and willing to learn are better equipped to navigate uncertainty and lead innovation.

By adopting a growth mindset, you can reframe challenges as opportunities for development, embrace the discomfort that comes with learning new technologies, and inspire your team to do the same. This mindset not only helps you stay relevant in a rapidly changing world but also enables you to push boundaries and explore uncharted territories in your industry.

Key Takeaway: Aligning Growth with the Future in a world where technology and leadership are rapidly evolving is key for success.

How to Build a Sustainable, Thriving Career in the Ever-Evolving IT Industry

The IT industry is dynamic and fast-growing, but its rapid pace also brings constant change. Technologies become obsolete quickly, new ones emerge, and industries are disrupted by innovation. As a mid-career professional, building a sustainable and thriving career in this environment requires foresight, adaptability, continuous learning, and a clear strategic vision.

My Journey: Lessons Learned

In my own journey as a mid-career software leader, I have faced many of these challenges firsthand. From leading Centers of Excellence (CoEs) to managing global programs and mentoring teams, I have gained a broad perspective on how to sustain a thriving career in such a fast-evolving space.

Commit to Lifelong Learning

One of the biggest threats to a mid-career professional is complacency. What worked for you five years ago may not work in the next five years, especially in IT. The shelf life of technical skills is becoming shorter, and staying relevant means committing to lifelong learning.

I recall enrolling in executive program and online courses to stay on top of new trends and technologies. For instance, when AI and machine learning started gaining traction, I made it a point to learn about these emerging technologies. This commitment to learning not only kept me relevant but also opened up new opportunities for growth.

Tip: Seek out opportunities to learn continuously. Explore new fields like AI, cybersecurity, and DevOps, which are becoming core components of the IT industry. Align these learnings with the larger trends in your field.

Develop Soft Skills Alongside Technical Expertise

As you move into leadership or more senior roles, technical skills alone will not sustain you. Soft skills like communication, emotional intelligence, and strategic thinking become critical.

When I transitioned from a purely technical role to a leadership role, I had to focus on building strong communication channels within teams and managing change effectively. One of my experiences was driving change in a high-pressure project while leading a CoE. Here, the technical solutions were important, but what really mattered was ensuring that every team member felt supported and motivated.

Tip: Work on honing your soft skills. Leadership roles require that you effectively influence, collaborate, and inspire teams. Focus on improving skills such as strategic thinking, team building, conflict resolution, and negotiation.

Embrace Innovation and Be Open to Change

The IT industry thrives on innovation, and resisting change is not an option. For mid-career professionals, this means being proactive about exploring new technologies and methodologies.

In my experience as a leader driving platformization and continuous improvement initiatives, I learned the importance of being ahead of the curve. We introduced gamification into daily routines to foster a culture of excellence. By embracing new ideas and encouraging the team to think creatively, we consistently delivered better outcomes.

Tip: Be the advocate for innovation within your organization. Whether through adopting new technologies or championing new processes, embracing change allows you to demonstrate leadership and adaptability.

Focus on Building a Network and Mentorship Relationships

Building a strong network is one of the most powerful tools for mid-career professionals. Relationships with colleagues, mentors, and industry leaders provide support, insight, and opportunities that may not be accessible otherwise.

Throughout my career, I have made it a point to build relationships with key stakeholders across different geographies and departments. As a Software CoE leader in Hyderabad, I led continuous improvement initiatives while developing a robust network across global CoEs. This helped not only in aligning cross-functional goals but also in establishing myself as a trusted leader across regions.

Moreover, mentorship has played a significant role in my growth. I have been fortunate to have mentors who challenged me to think beyond the scope of my role and embrace new opportunities.

Tip: Prioritize networking, both within and outside of your organization. Attend industry conferences, engage in forums, and build relationships with people who inspire you. If you do not have a mentor, find one—and be prepared to become a mentor yourself.

Align Personal Growth with Industry Trends

Perhaps the most critical element of building a sustainable career in IT is aligning your personal growth with industry trends. IT is a forward-looking industry, and your career path must be, too.

In my role as a product leader, I have seen firsthand how companies that fail to adapt to industry shifts risk becoming irrelevant. To avoid this fate, I have consistently sought out new technologies and market trends, anticipating where the industry is headed.

Tip: Keep an eye on industry reports, publications, and thought leaders to understand the trends shaping the IT landscape. Identify which technologies or practices will have the biggest impact on your career or organization, and start building the skills and experience to lead in those areas.

Key Takeaway is Future-Proofing Your Career for Long-Term Success

Building a sustainable and thriving career in the ever-evolving IT industry is not about mastering a specific technology but learning, adapting, and applying new technologies in your area of work.

Conclusion: Your Journey Ahead

As I reach the final words of this book, I find myself reflecting not just on the lessons I have shared but also on the countless stories of mid-career professionals—people like you— who navigate the crossroads of ambition, stagnation, and transformation. This journey, as challenging as it may seem, is one of the most rewarding undertakings you will ever embark on.

From the very first page, my goal has been to walk alongside you as a guide and confidant, sharing the insights, strategies, and stories that shaped my career and those of others in the IT world. Let's take a moment to revisit where we have been together and look ahead to where you are going.

Recognizing and Navigating the Mid-Career Plateau

We began by acknowledging the often overlooked reality of mid-career plateaus—a stage where many professionals feel stuck despite their experience and accomplishments. Whether it is the fear of change or uncertainty about what is next, this phase can feel like an insurmountable wall.

But here is what we uncovered: the plateau is not the end of the road. It is a pivotal moment—a signpost urging you to reflect, recalibrate, and reignite your career. By understanding these challenges, you have already taken the first critical step toward transformation.

Defining Your Career Direction

Clarity became the cornerstone of our next step. Crafting your vision, mission, and goals is not just an exercise; it is your blueprint for success. Think back to the moments when you visualized your dream career, aligned it with your personal life, and began shaping a roadmap to get there.

Your career direction is your compass, and your personal brand is the vessel that will carry you forward. As we explored strategies for building visibility and influence, I hope you recognized the immense power you hold to position yourself as a leader in the IT industry. Remember, the world notices those who make an effort to be noticed.

Building Leadership and Managing Teams

Leadership is not just about managing teams; it is about inspiring them. Whether transitioning from an individual contributor to a leader or fostering high-performing teams, we discussed the importance of traits like empathy, resilience, and the ability to lead by example.

Continuous learning emerged as a recurring theme—not just as a necessity but as a mindset. The IT industry evolves at breakneck speed, and staying relevant requires curiosity, adaptability, and a willingness to learn skills outside your comfort zone. Think of the certifications you have considered, the books you have earmarked, or the mentorship opportunities you have identified. They are your tools for growth.

Overcoming Challenges and Pushing Boundaries

This was perhaps the most personal part of our journey together. Growth does not come from staying comfortable; it comes from venturing into the unknown. The stories of professionals who pushed beyond their comfort zones were a testament to the transformative power of courage and determination.

And what about setbacks? We explored how failures are not the end—they are stepping stones. Every career stumble, every "no" you have faced, is preparing you for a future "yes". Resilience, as we discussed, is your armor in this battle. Building it requires embracing failure, learning from it, and moving forward with renewed focus.

Long-Term Success and Organizational Impact

As leaders, your responsibility extends beyond personal growth to influencing the organizations you serve. By fostering a culture of excellence and driving innovation, you have the power to shape not just your career but the future of your company.

Future-proofing your career means staying ahead of trends, anticipating challenges, and aligning your growth with the ever-evolving tech landscape. The IT industry rewards those who dare to innovate and think long-term. You are now equipped to be one of those visionaries.

The Road Ahead

So, where do you go from here?

This book is not just a collection of chapters; it is a call to action. Each page has armed you with the tools, strategies, and insights you need to craft the next chapter of your career. But reading is only the beginning. True transformation happens when you act.

Start small. Reflect on the key lessons that resonated with you the most. Is it redefining your goals, stepping out of your comfort zone, or pursuing a leadership role? Identify one area to focus on this month and commit to making progress.

Remember, your journey is not linear. There will be highs and lows, victories and setbacks. But every step, no matter how small, brings you closer to the career and life you have envisioned.

A Final Word on Resilience and Leadership

Let me leave you with this: Leadership begins with leading yourself. As you grow into the leader you are meant to be, embrace the principles of adaptability, resilience and courage

(ARC framework). These traits will not only define your career but also leave an indelible mark on the people and organizations you touch.

Your story is still unfolding. The fact that you are holding this book means you have already decided to rise above challenges and lead yourself towards a brighter future.

So, take that next step. Write your vision, push your boundaries, and build the legacy you are capable of creating. The road ahead is yours to conquer. And I, for one, cannot wait to see where it leads you.

Your Turn

Before you close this book, I invite you to reflect: What is the one action you will take today to Rise and Lead? Write it down, commit to it, and begin the transformation you have been waiting for.

Because your journey is not just about rising – it is about inspiring others to rise alongside you. And that, my friend, is the true essence of leadership.

So go on—rise, lead, and make your mark. The world needs you, and I know you are ready.

____

____

____

____

____

____

____

____

____

____

Acknowledgments

As I reflect on the journey that led to this book, I am filled with gratitude for the many people who have played an instrumental role in shaping my career and inspiring me to share my journey. This book is not just the culmination of my experiences; it is a testament to the support, guidance, and encouragement I have received from so many remarkable individuals along the way.

To my mentors: Your wisdom and unwavering belief in my potential have been a guiding light during moments of uncertainty. You have not only shared your knowledge but also inspired me to push boundaries and pursue excellence. Your mentorship has left an indelible mark on my journey, and I owe much of my growth to your invaluable lessons.

To my colleagues and managers: You have been my collaborators, challengers, and motivators. The countless projects, brainstorming sessions, and shared successes (and failures) have enriched my perspective and equipped me with the skills to navigate the complexities of leadership and career transitions. Thank you for your camaraderie and trust, which have been the foundation of many milestones in my professional life.

To my friends: Your encouragement, listening ears, and words of advice have been a source of strength during both the highs and the lows. Whether cheering me on or simply being there to share a laugh, your presence has been a vital part of my journey.

To my wife Sandhya: You are my unwavering pillars of support. Your love, patience, and understanding have given me the courage to dream big and the resilience to overcome challenges. and to my childrens (Varun and Ishanvi) you are my greatest strength and energy. Each chapter of this book carries a piece of your influence, and it is with immense gratitude that I dedicate these words to all of you. Thank you for being part of my story and for helping me find the courage to write it.

This book is as much yours as it is mine, and I hope it serves as a tribute to the profound impact you have had on my life.

About the Author

Nagaraju Siddam (Nag), from a middle-class family and the first in his family circle to pursue higher education, completed his engineering from National Institute of Technology (NIT) Warangal and later earned an Executive MBA from the Indian School of Business (ISB). With over two decades in the tech industry, Nag has held multiple global roles, led teams across continents, and established Centers of Excellence in high-tech organizations. He has successfully transitioned critical projects from global sites to India, driving product continuity, operational excellence, and growth. In Rise and Lead: Reignite, Reinvent, and Succeed in Your Mid-Career Journey, Nag shares his story of overcoming challenges and transforming setbacks into opportunities, offering practical strategies to help mid-career professionals reignite their purpose, break through stagnation, and step into impactful leadership roles.

References

Reach out to me over LinkedIn: https://www.linkedin.com/in/nagaraju-siddam/

Books for reference:

1. Attitude is Everything by Jeff keller

2. Growth Mindset by Carol Dweck

3. Ikigai – Hector Garcia

4. 10x easier than 2x-by Benjamin Hardy and Dan Sullivan

5. Atomic Habits by James Clear by Simon Sinek.

6. The Power of Your Subconscious Mind by Joseph Murphy.

7. 7 habit of highly effective people by stephen covey"The Ultimate Secret of Total Self-Confidence" book by Dr. Robert Anthony

8. The 22 Immutable Laws of Branding by Al Ries and Laura RiesTwo Birds in a Tree by Ram Nidumolu

9.   The 5AM Club – Robin Sharma

10. 10X Rule by Grant Cardone

11. Leadership Wisdom – Robin Sharma Cues by Vanessa Van Edwards